The Church In Crisis

The Church In Crisis

Ron Auch
with John Cronce

New Leaf Press

FIRST EDITION
1990

Copyright © 1990 by New Leaf Press, Inc. All rights reserved. No part of this book may be used or reproduced in any manner whatsoever without written permission of the publisher except in the case of brief quotations in articles and reviews. For information write: New Leaf Press, Inc., P.O. Box 311, Green Forest, AR 72638.

Library of Congress Catalog Card Number:
90-61176
ISBN: 0-89221-181-4

Cover photo: J & J Tiner Photographs

This book is also being published in a similar form under the title "Pentecostals In Crisis."

DEDICATION

This book is dedicated to the Church of Jesus Christ. "The" greatest tool for completing His work.

Contents

Acknowledgements 7
Introduction 9
1 An Answer in the Past 15
2 The Power Encounter 29
3 Cisterns That Hold No Water 39
4 Today's Church: Limited To Man's Abilities 55
5 Rebuilding the Ancient Boundaries 71
6 The Fall of the Slight Tower 83
7 Coming to God in Truth 93
8 Your Concept of God 101
9 God Working in Us 111
10 Doing The Right Thing The Wrong Way 115
11 Diligently Seeking God 133
12 Communicating Like Christ 143
13 The Praying Church 157

ACKNOWLEDGEMENTS

"It was the best of times, it was the worst of times." That's how Charles Dickens began his classic *A Tale of Two Cities*, and that's also how I am tempted to begin my humble literary effort. Certainly writing this book has been the best of times. It is the fulfillment of a vision for God's Church that He birthed in my heart through prayer over a number of years.

However, writing a book must, by definition it seems, include the worst of times. It was during these most arduous moments that I felt especially privileged to have the support and input of several very talented individuals who have worked behind the scenes with me before. Joe Lehman, computer genius extraordinaire, is to be congratulated for his patience and teaching abilities. Not only did he teach me how to efficiently use a new computer system, he also managed to convince me that the same system was out to get me. (It took a lot of convincing). Thanks, Joe. I must also express my gratitude to Dan Cypcar, an engineering major at the University of Wisconsin-Milwaukee who has since graduated. The many hours he sacrificed, even when it was inconvenient, as was the case the week before his final exams, were a treasure to me, as he introduced me to the computer system that the earliest drafts of this book were processed on. Computers are here to stay, aren't they, Dan? (But you still don't have to like them!)

I would also like to extend my special thanks to the folks who read manuscripts of this book in various stages of completion. Joe Lehman played a special role here ("It might be clear to you because you wrote it, but, as a reader, I'm a little unclear about..."). Similarly I want to thank Sue Smolinksi who waded through the entire first draft of this book in one sitting. Thanks, Sue, for your input, encouragement and prayers. As usual, they were a deep, rich blessing to me.

Saving the best for last, I must thank my Lord and Saviour, Jesus Christ. I owe everything I am to Him (sometimes in spite of my feeble, frail, human self). He really gave me the concepts for this book, so in that sense I must defer authorship to Him. It is my greatest hope and prayer that others will be blessed by these concepts as I was when I was first taught them by Him.

INTRODUCTION

I felt guilty for not keeping up with the news. I had been very busy for a couple weeks and hadn't listened to TV or radio news, to say nothing of reading a newspaper or news magazine. I was rather tired, but instead of going to bed, I clicked on the TV and opened a window. A pleasant summer breeze flowed through the room as I headed for the overstuffed chair opposite the television. I gazed outside at the clear starlit sky while a used car dealer peddled his dubious wares on the set. For a few seconds, I sat in awe of the very stars Abraham had gazed at when he was promised that he would be the father of many nations. Suddenly, my attention was snatched back to the television as I heard the news anchorman describing the evening's lead story.

"A local man nearly became a victim of satanic cultists today," he said. My mouth went dry and a slight chill ran up and down my spine. I had been hearing many stories about the rise of satanism in our country, but these stories always came from Los Angeles or New York, some place a respectable distance from my home and family. But this story took place in Milwaukee, the nearest big city to my home in Kenosha. As I stared in amazement, the newscaster described how a woman lured a man into her apartment. Once inside, he went into the bathroom to investigate a noise. When he walked in, two other young women jumped out from behind the shower curtain, one of them brandishing an axe. She missed him with her first swipe, but slashed his forehead on her second. Since it wasn't a square hit, he was able to beat a hasty retreat, though badly bleeding, while his pursuers chanted "Redrum!" as they had seen an axe murderer do in a movie ("redrum" is "murder" spelled backwards). The prospective human sacrifice escaped to alert authorities and to get medical attention. In the end, the women were arrested and their victim received fifty stitches.

The grisly news report slapped me in the face, reminding me again of our nation's plight. During police questioning, these three women rather cavalierly admitted that they had planned to drain their victim's blood from his body, dismember him, and eat his kidneys as part of a satanic ritual. Indeed, satanism is growing. I have been told by youth evangelists that it is reaching into our high schools. Many teenagers are looking for something—something powerful and exciting. They're finding that—and much more than they bargained for, I suspect—in devil worship. It is also booming on college campuses. A college student who attends the same church as my family and I told me his roommate was dabbling with the occult. He said this young man went about their dormitory collecting small samples of blood with which he painted a pentagram on a ouija board to summon Satan. When he and some others succeeded in contacting a demon who claimed to be Satan, it possessed (at least temporarily) one of the participants. But instead of frightening them, it served to further motivate them to seek out this dark realm and even encourage others to join them.

To be sure, our adversary, the devil, as a roaring lion, walks about in the twentieth century United States. His influence on people is growing.

One of the three young women involved in the aforementioned murder attempt claimed that she had an additional reason for being involved. She was convinced that in a previous life she was the mother of the mysterious mass murderer Jack the Ripper, who plagued London's east end during the latter half of the nineteenth century. She claimed that she wanted to commit a murder as ghastly as one committed by her supposed son to demonstrate her love and affection for him. Mystical beliefs like this woman's are also becoming popular in our country. Most major book chains now have an aisle prominently designated "New Age." Major themes in these books inspired by the New Age movement include reincarnation, out-of-body experiences, and contact with spirits. Many of these books also proclaim that there are no such things as either right or wrong, insisting that there are instead simply different ideas, all competing with each other. An increasing number of Americans are turning to this kind of mysticism for spiritual guidance and are rejecting the Christian Church for insight into these matters.

In the days that followed, the bizarre attempted homicide filled the newspapers and was even reported by CNN, the national TV news network. As new facts surfaced, I continued to ponder the state of our country. Some people have told me that man has been wronging his neighbor since the murder of innocent Abel at the hands of his brother Cain and that things aren't any worse than they've always been. They say that things only look worse now because news, mostly bad news, can be transmitted more rapidly and over greater distances than ever before. I am grateful to be reminded of these points because they are true, at least to an extent. Yes, "all have sinned and fallen short of the glory of God" since man's exile from Eden. That's why Jesus came to die for us. There has never been a utopia, a society without corruption, since the fall of man. It is equally true that our culture possesses the most advanced technology in the history of mankind; and consequently, we are more informed about the happenings in our world. Yet these truths do not alter the fact that the moral climate of our nation and of the entire Western world has deteriorated greatly in the course of the last several decades.

Law enforcement agencies across the country agree that the number of crimes committed in our nation is increasing. I am aware of the theory which postulates that this increase is due to an overall population increase (i.e., more people means more bankers, more farmers, more criminals, etc.). However, this cannot explain our situation. The numerical rise in killings (not just satanically-inspired ones), for example, has outstripped the rise in total population.

Furthermore, the nature of the crimes has changed. Earlier, I referred to Jack the Ripper, the unidentified cutthroat dubbed thusly by a reporter at the height of the legendary 1888 murder spree. What gave the Ripper his reputation, great enough to survive to this very day, was not that he killed. People living in the impoverished Whitechapel area of London were no strangers to the crime of murder. What was strange and frightening about him was that he viciously mutilated the bodies of his victims, apparently with no provocation. Also, since they were not robbed, there was apparently no potential for profit. He seemed to be one who killed just for the pleasure of the deed. That was rare.

In more recent times, though, such crimes have become less and less rare. Across our land, police departments are glutted with unsolved serial murders. Only a few murderers like Charles Mansen and John Wayne Gacey have been apprehended. I have no wish to idealize or romanticize the past, but it just seems that the wicked heart of man has grown even more wicked. People are indulging in murder more and more with less and less provocation. We have reached the point where we are no longer scandalized when we hear an account of a lone gunman marching into a fast-food restaurant and arbitrarily gunning down the patrons.

Murder is not the only crime on the rise. Illegal drug traffic has reached epic proportions in our nation and shows no signs of declining. It really exploded in the 1960s when the hippies and other young people began exploring drugs. Since then, things have only grown worse. Users are still largely young people—but they are becoming younger and younger. Grammar schools are now having to launch their own wars on drugs, just as the high schools have been forced to do. Children in our society are being mercilessly exploited and are becoming addicted to drugs before they even reach adolescence. But drug abuse is no longer limited to the young or to the people on the wrong side of the tracks. Highly successful businessmen are also becoming enslaved to drugs and are in the process of destroying themselves and their families.

Families are, to say the least, greatly threatened. An exploding divorce rate is thrusting an increasing number of single parents into a pressure cooker world where they must maintain a job or career and raise their children at the same time. In many instances, children are neglected, resulting in emotionally impoverished children who go on to develop emotional and psychological disturbances. Meanwhile, other couples are staying together grudgingly hopefully to benefit their children. The children, however, find little solace in warring parents who at best maintain cold civility toward one another. These children, too, suffer.

As the family structure has crumbled, so have morals. Sexual contact outside of marriage has been growing in acceptance and popularity since the 1960s. Consequently, "unwanted" pregnancies have resulted, and a corrupt generation has decided to separate itself from the consequences of its sin by murdering the unborn by millions. Increasingly, abstinence until marriage is looked upon as something puritanical, anachronistic, and idealistic. Moreover, casual attitudes regarding sexual contact have grown beyond heterosexuality. Homosexuality and lesbianism are being paraded in our streets with gay pride marches, many of which have the endorsement and approval of our legislators. This kind of deviance continues to be defended in spite of the AIDS epidemic that this perversion has unleashed.

In short, our nation is in crisis. But even more shocking, as we will see in the following chapters, is the state of today's Church. Though murder is not increasing in the Church, studies indicate that alcoholism, divorce, fornication, and adultery are rising at such an alarming rate that it won't be long before the saints are rivaling the world's expertise at sin. It is sad but true that at the hour when a world in crisis needs the Church most, at the hour when it looks more likely than ever that Jesus will be returning, the Church is in crisis.

CHAPTER ONE

AN ANSWER IN THE PAST

> "Those who fail to learn from history are doomed to repeat it."
> —Unknown

The Church is in crisis. It is an unpopular thing to say, but it is true. However, my message goes beyond this simple statement. If my message were nothing more, it could be contained in a tract as easily as in a book. We are in crisis, but we are by no means destined to remain in crisis. There is, as we will see, a solution. But we must understand the nature of our problem before we can discuss a solution. To understand both our problem and the solution to it, it will be necessary for us to take a trip backward in time, for, as we will see, only by learning from the past can we change the present.

NEXT STOP: JERUSALEM, A.D. 33

That day began much like every other day in all respects. It was the day of Pentecost and, therefore, Jews and converts to Judaism had flocked to Jerusalem from all over the empire to honor and celebrate the holiday. While preparations were being made for the day's activities all over Jerusalem, the followers of Jesus were nowhere to be found. They were meeting in an upper room, praying and fellowshipping as they had been doing ever since Jesus had instructed them to do so before departing into heaven. He had told them to tarry in Jerusalem to await the Holy Spirit, a Counselor who would be with them forever, and He had told them they would receive power when the Spirit came on them. Suddenly, the room was filled with the sound of a violent wind—but there was no wind. Then what appeared like tongues of fire came to rest on each one of them and they began speaking in languages strange to their ears. However, some foreigners outside heard the commotion and they recognized the multilingual cries as praises to God in their own languages. Others became interested in the spectacle, and a crowd began to form. Some, like the foreigners, were astonished while others just dismissed it as the babbling of drunks. Finally, one of the disciples, Simon Peter, came out and explained the wonder taking place. He hadn't spent weeks or even hours preparing an eloquent message; he was shooting from the hip. He clearly explained how this phenomenon was a fulfillment of Scripture, going on to explain that Jesus' life, death, and resurrection were all for the atonement of their sins. That day three thousand repented, believed, and were added to the Church.

Most Christians can quickly identify the miracles at work that day: the believers' ability to speak in languages they didn't know, the sound of a wind where there was no wind, and something like flames hovering over the disciples. But one miracle often goes overlooked: the three thousand conversions. It is important to realize that they weren't just temporary commitments that expired in a few days or weeks. They were "added to the Church" as well as being saved. To use an aphorism, I'm sure any pastor or evangelist today would give his eyeteeth to see such results. Curiously, the early believers saw these results in spite of the fact that no one planned or promoted such an outreach. Since it was unplanned, there was no designated speaker until the last moment, and consequently, no laboriously prepared sermon. They were totally unprepared by our standards. In fact, by our standards they were doomed to failure (a fact which should cause us to reconsider our standards). Something happened that day that brought people to God in a quality and quantity unseen in our present day, even with all our education, technology, and comparative wealth.

A GREAT AWAKENING FROM GREAT SLUMBER

Whatever yielded such fantastic results back in Jerusalem was not limited to the ancient world or to Eastern culture. The last couple centuries of Western history are full of similar occurrences. Frequently these incidents took place under the leadership of men who seemed the least likely for such a role. One such man was George Whitefield, the dynamic British preacher of the eighteenth century. As a child growing up in 1720s Britain, he had no church affiliation. Like many adolescents today, he was afflicted with the most profane speech, and he lied almost as much as he swore. His formative years were punctuated by his roguish exploits and his unhappy family life. By the time he was seventeen, George's parents ended their volatile marriage in divorce. George was sent off to Oxford in the hopes that he might yet make something of himself. However, Oxford was not the solution for George. Life there provided a very solitary existence for him, and, in his loneliness, he began pondering a subject he probably thought he never would: religion. This new interest seems to have surprised Whitefield as much as it had those around him. Yet he pushed past the questioning glances of those around him and determined in his heart to seek out God, prostrating himself on the floor for days and weeks at a time. Finally, George's prayers were answered when he came to understand the basic message of the Gospels and what it means to be born again. He wrote of that moment, "Oh what joy—joy unspeakable—joy full and big with glory was my soul filled with when the weight of my sin came off." But that wasn't the end. It was just the beginning.

Whitefield became a preacher at the age of twenty-one. When he preached, he preached about the living God he had met. He didn't orate about things he studied with his mind but didn't know with his heart. His preaching was so powerful that during his first sermon, people were so convicted that they were said to have been driven mad. The church was jammed full of repenting sinners. Whitefield's success was partially attributed to his eloquence and commanding voice, both of which were envied by popular actors of the day. He was also a very creative man. For example, on one occasion, he preached a sermon on the topic, "It is appointed once unto man to die" while standing on a gallows. As he was warning his hearers that they, too, would die and face judgment, a man cried out and died. Shortly after, so did another. The angel of death himself seemed to be visiting them. Needless to say, the imminency of death was made quite real to those people, but even more so was the reality of God, as real and as conscious as they themselves were. They realized that God was not a mute, impotent God of religious rhetoric who refuses to involve himself in the affairs of men. That day they were confronted with the Almighty of the Bible, banishing from their minds the insipid, distant God of established religion.

It soon became apparent that a great religious fervor was blazing through the British Isles as preachers like Whitefield and John Wesley seemed to be coming out of the woodwork, each preaching the gospel of salvation, each receiving droves of adult converts. But it wasn't confined to Great Britain. It began to spread, and nowhere was it needed more than in the North American colonies.

New England in the 1720s and early 1730s was a little bit like the United States of the 1960s and early 1970s—and like our nation today to a lesser extent. Children rebelled against their parents in a way that was more bold and inflexible than anyone remembered ever happening before. They refused to attend church, stayed out late, drinking, and carousing. Church records from that period chronicle births occurring very shortly after many marriages, particularly among very young couples, leading us to conclude that they became quite promiscuous. Their parents' vocal objections were partly ignored. These parents attended church services regularly, but failed to practice what they preached. Their churches had lapsed into a rather hypocritical state, fraught with inner strife and lethargy. Like the Church today, they were in crisis.

Then when people in America least expected it (and most needed it), a spirit of repentance and endearment to God swept through their land just as it had in Britain. Jonathan Edwards was one of the most prominent leaders of this movement. He is best known today for his sermon, "Sinners in the Hands of an Angry God," in which he told his listeners, "God...dreadfully abhors you...[and He] dangles you over the precipice much as one would dangle a spider over the flame." Such statements are rather hard to swallow. In fact, it represents a seriously flawed theology (i.e., God does not dreadfully abhor us as Edwards supposed), as well as a dismal outlook on life. What's more I would expect that such statements would be rejected by their era's "hippies," who would reason that if God hated them and was going to get even with them in the next life anyway, they might as well keep living it up in this one. It seems that it would be equally ineffective with their stuffy parents who felt their religion had already made them acceptable to God and who might brand the sermon a demonstration of scare tactics, fanaticism, as a malicious insult, or any combination of the three.

In spite of many criticisms, the cold hearts of old and young alike were moved during the service in which he preached the sermon. Some people clamped onto the backs of the pews in front of them until their knuckles turned white. Many screamed, others wept and moaned. They were horrified by the waste that their lives had been and were repulsed by their lifelong rejection of God Almighty for the fleeting pleasures of this world. More importantly, they repented and believed. The kingdom of heaven was at hand. Edwards' church, cold, impersonal, infested with strife, hypocrisy, and divisiveness, was completely transformed. Parents and children reconciled their differences. Tears flowed at every service. Some wept in repentance, others in pity for the unregenerate, while still others wept out of sheer joy as they heard the Word of God.

This "Great Awakening" is truly intriguing, even today (or perhaps especially today). Some might say Whitefield's success was a product of his own giftedness, yet I am convinced that something else was at work that would explain the deaths of two of his hearers as he preached a sermon on the imminency of death and judgment. Likewise, some might attribute the results of Jonathan Edwards to theatrics and scare tactics. However, it is a well-known fact in historical and literary circles that his poor sight required Edwards to bury his face in the pages of his sermon—which he read verbatim in a monotone. Somehow the picture of such a sermon so delivered does not stir my heart. No, I must maintain that there was something more which led those people to do a complete about-face with gut-wrenching conviction and emotion. It was something more than a nice preacher preaching a nice sermon, a nice choir singing a nice song, something more than nice people attending a nice church.

ON INTO THE NINETEENTH CENTURY

Unfortunately, with the passing of that generation and the rise of a new one, the phenomenon was extinguished. By the beginning of the nineteenth century, a mist of spiritual slumber descended on the young republic. Organized religion became lukewarm and the target of criticism by intellectuals. Rationalism was being imported from France, and it was becoming an increasingly popular philosophy. It essentially limited all of reality to that which could be perceived by the five senses of man. This tended to eliminate God from one's view of reality, or at least to limit Him so much that He might just as well be ignored.

Moreover, many who remained in the nation's churches blended rationalism with Christianity. As a result Christianity largely became limited to what man could do and perceive naturally. Still, there were some in the Church who sensed a need in the human soul that could not be met by the reasoning and intellectualism of finite man. Two such people were James McGreedy and Barton Stone, both Presbyterian ministers. In the summer of 1800, they traveled from their home state, North Carolina, to Kentucky where they held a four-day meeting. What resulted was remarkable. Stone wrote, "It baffled description. Many, very many, fell down as men slain in battle and continued for hours together in an apparently breathless and motionless state, sometimes for a few moments reviving and exhibiting symptoms of life by deep groan or a piercing shriek, or a prayer for mercy fearfully uttered" (Harold Fischer, *Reviving Revivals*, Gospel Publishing House, 1950, p. 166).

I am aware that many today (as back then) view such reports with great skepticism. Some are inclined to attribute these events to intoxication, a desire for entertainment, or even to a nervous breakdown. But none of these explanations can account for the salvation of thousands who flocked to the meeting from as far as one hundred miles away (without automobiles, trains, or airplanes). Neither do they account for their singular love for God. It was a passion unrivaled by a love of the things of this world. Those new believers cherished their Lord and Saviour like nothing else. "No person seemed to wish to go home," McGreedy wrote. "Hunger and sleep seemed to affect nobody—eternal things were the vast concerns...Sober professors who had been communicants for many years were now lying prostrate on the ground crying out in such language as this, 'Oh, how I would have despised any person a few days ago who would have acted as I am doing now! But I cannot help it!'" (Lewis A. Drummond, *The Awakening That Must Come*, Boardman Press, 1978, pp. 15-16).

There were no nearby lodgings to accommodate the growing multitudes, but that didn't deter people from coming. They just brought tents and bedrolls along with them and camped out, giving birth to the first camp meeting.

The camp meetings caught on, igniting the frontier. Interestingly, they were not denominationally restricted. Baptist revivalism first began in those days, and the Methodists and Presbyterians held just as many such meetings. One believer reported, "At one time, I saw at least five hundred swept down in a moment as if a battery of a thousand guns opened upon them, and then immediately followed shrieks and shouts that rent the very heavens" (Mendall Taylor, *Exploring Evangelism*, Beacon Hill Press, 1964, p.142).

Like the first Great Awakening, the second Great Awakening was a time of remarkable church growth as well as deep spiritual commitment. Like the days of the New Testament Church, it was a time of divinely-inspired growth during which God used men for great purposes and yet, those men were neither able nor willing to take credit for what happened. Although those people took part in leading the movement, their abilities, albeit God-given, did not alone accomplish what took place. What happened was beyond man's abilities and his understanding. Something else was involved.

Unfortunately, when the generation which first experienced this passed on, their successors did not share their vision, and the flames of excitement were reduced to a smoldering nostalgia. By the time the third generation arose, the old way had expired completely.

AWAKENING IN THE TWENTIETH CENTURY

As the United States marched into the new century, it stood in awe of itself. Once primarily agrarian, the nation was rapidly industrializing. People were flocking from the farms to the cities, where men like J.P. Morgan and Andrew Carnegie made their legendary fortunes. Carnegie boasted that he had begun with nothing as an Irish immigrant and that any pauper could become a tycoon if he would just work as hard and think as creatively as he had. Things were looking pretty good back on the farms, too. New farm machinery was constantly being introduced, making farming increasingly more efficient. The end result was that even though there were fewer farmers, the nation was producing more food per capita than ever before because its farmers were better equipped to face the challenge than ever before. What's more, the continental United States, composed of the current forty-eight states, was crisscrossed with a network of railroads, making quick, comfortable travel to just about anywhere in the nation possible. At the same time, medical science was continuously making incredible breakthroughs. The same things were going on in varying degrees in Europe, and man was becoming smug. Very smug.

Heady scientists were explaining man's existence as an evolutionary fluke, and these scientists were being listened to and praised by intellectuals. And when did man evolve a soul, making him unique from the animals? Was there ever a creature that was half-man and half-animal that was denied a soul? Did God refuse a soul to a creature that was ninety-nine percent man and one percent animal? Such questions were never asked because part of the assumption was that man was not inherently special, but just an advanced animal; the assumption underlying this was there was no God.

Many were convinced man was on his way to creating utopia, that he was evolving beyond violence, poverty, and discord. After seeing man create the long-dreamed-of flying machine, they were convinced he could create anything he dreamed of, given enough time. His technology and science, feeding off each other, would create a new Eden (one without a God to subordinate to). They considered war a thing of the past and certainly didn't envision mechanized slaughter in a global war by 1914. In some ways, it was very much like our world today. Yet, there were those in and out of the Church who realized that there was a vacuum deep within the human heart. Christians began holding more prayer meetings than they had in a long time—and that's when the same phenomenon visited the world again.

Wales was the first to witness this revival phenomenon. It was quite similar to the earlier occurrences during the first and second Great Awakenings. As tens of thousands were saved, churches all over Wales became crowded where formerly attendance was sparse. Again, there were souls *added to the Church*, their testimonies resounding well into the 1930s. The great harvest left some areas of society devastated. Many taverns, for example, were forced to close their doors as alcoholism plummeted by fifty percent. Police departments were bored like never before since few crimes were being committed.

As with all these instances, the best way to get a grasp of this one is by examining the reports of on-the-spot witnesses. One of the most prestigious witnesses was William T. Stead, renowned as the editor of the *Pall Mall Gazette*. In a newspaper interview with the *London Methodist Times*, Stead was asked if he dreaded the revival coming his way. He replied, "Dread is not the right word. Awe expresses my sentiment better. For you are in the presence of the unknown...You have read ghost stories and can imagine what you would feel if you were alone at midnight in the haunted chamber of some old castle and you heard the slow and stealthy step stealing along the corridor where a visitor from another world was said to walk. If you go to South Wales and watch the revival, you will feel pretty much like that. There is something there from the other world. You cannot say whence it came or whither it is going, but it moves and lives and reaches out for you all the time. You see men and women go down in sobbing agony before your eyes as the invisible Hand clutches at their heart, and you shudder."

When it struck in the United States, its effect on society was no less profound than it was across the sea. In 1905, pastors in Atlantic City stated that only fifty people were left in the community of sixty thousand who did not profess salvation. "The mayor of Denver declared a day of prayer; by 10:00 a.m., churches were filled; at 11:30, almost every store closed; twelve thousand attended prayer meetings in downtown theaters and halls" (J. Edwin Orr, *The Flaming Tongue*, Moody Press, 1968, p.107). Church growth was astonishing all over the country. First Baptist Church in Peducah, Kentucky, an average church, accepted one thousand new members in two months (Mary Stewart Relfe, Ph.D., *Cure of All Ills*, League of Prayer, 1988, p.99).

A good example of the meetings of this time is the series of meetings conducted at 312 Azusa Street in Los Angeles. These meetings did not take place in the most beautiful church in town. Quite the contrary, they were held in an old, unattractive, two-story frame building which had been used most recently as a livery stable and tenement house, which some compared inside and out to a barn. Inside this humble shack there was no gorgeously-garbed choir, nor was there a finely-tuned orchestra. What's more, no hand bills were distributed, nor was there any other kind of public advertising employed to promote the meetings.

The response to the altar calls was enormous even though the calls were given simply and matter-of-factly, without coaxing, cajoling, or psychological wheedling. As in Wales and elsewhere in the world, visions and uncanny discernment were reported, but there was more. Those in attendance began reporting miraculous healings. They claimed that physical laws were virtually being bent. A great many reported speaking in languages they didn't know, as in the Book of Acts, giving rise to the Pentecostal movement. One report told how a foreign-born journalist recognized an utterance in his native tongue and understood it to be a precise account of sins he committed and was sure nobody knew about. He ended up getting saved, as well as being fired for offering his editors an impartial report of the revival instead of the deriding article they demanded of him (Dr. William J. Menzies, *Anointed to Serve*, Gospel Publishing House, 1971, p.53).

IN SUMMARY

Throughout history it has happened in the Church, and it is the heritage of most of today's Christian denominations. When people like the ancient Jews or Western intellectuals in latter days thought the Christians were on their way out, it happened. When society was fraught with moral ills like eighteenth-century New England was, it happened. When Christians were lacking commitment and joy in their walks with God, it happened. In times like our own, it has happened. When it happened church attendance exploded—with some churches more than doubling within one year. Even more breathtaking, the moral quality of the congregations skyrocketed as was the case in Jonathan Edwards' church. Backbiting, gloomy members became an endangered species. When it happened, God used people like the nearsighted Jonathan Edwards, gifted with a monotonous voice, and the worldly, unchurched pagan, George Whitefield. Astonishing things took place:

things that man wasn't prepared for, didn't engineer, and frequently things he would never be capable of doing anyway. Men and women were saved in such a deep, profound way that nothing else mattered to them, not even hunger and sleep, as was the case in the first camp meetings. The Church was at Her best. Her members were at their best in the area of loving the Lord with all their heart, soul, strength, and their neighbors as themselves. The Church was at Her best in fulfilling the Great Commission. It was this divine phenomenon that God sent to rescue the Church and individuals from crisis. And it is this which we must examine.

CHAPTER TWO

THE POWER ENCOUNTER

> "Without experience, nothing can be known sufficiently."
> —Roger Bacon

"Meanwhile, Saul was still breathing out murderous threats against the Lord's disciples. He went to the high priest and asked him for letters to the synagogues in Damascus, so that if he found any there who belonged to the Way, whether men or women, he might take them prisoners to Jerusalem. As he neared Damascus on his journey, suddenly a light from heaven flashed around him. He fell to the ground and heard a voice say to him, 'Saul, Saul, why do you persecute me?' 'Who are you, Lord?' Saul asked. 'I am Jesus, whom you are persecuting,' he replied. 'Now get up and go into the city, and you will be told what you must do'" (Acts 9:1-6).

Saul was one of those people who was anything but

average. You know the type. Even as a youth, he had things a little better than the other Jewish kids. He wasn't schooled in the synagogue with the other children by some generic rabbi. Instead, he was instructed by Gamaliel, one of the most famous and revered rabbis in Israel. It was like being taught physics by Albert Einstein. Any boy in Saul's position was headed in only one direction: up! From childhood on, Saul seemed destined to have his name etched in the *Who's Who in Jewish Synagogues* scrolls.

Saul's climb up the ladder of success was abruptly halted when he ran head-on with the resurrected Messiah whose followers he was persecuting in a blood-thirsty exhibition of Jewish zealotry. Something happened on that road to Damascus that caused this young up-and-coming pharisee to forsake all the popularity and respect he had struggled so hard to gain.

Saul experienced what I have termed a **power encounter** with Christ. When he met Christ, it turned his world upside down. The course of his life turned 180-degrees. By this I don't mean that he only experienced God's redemptive grace. More than that took place. Yes, his sins were forgiven, but he also experienced a thorough transformation which reversed his concept of right and wrong. His hopes, his hates, his dreams, and his desires all radically changed. This was proven when he turned his back on all that he had spent his life attaining so he could—of all things— wander the length and breadth of the Roman Empire preaching about salvation through the same Jesus he had formerly persecuted with such ferocity. It was something none of his contemporaries could fathom. It is also, unfortunately, an experience which many Christians are losing sight of today.

THE WAY THINGS SHOULD BE

In spite of the condition of the Church today, the power encounter has hallmarked the Church. A review of the last chapter will demonstrate that it was at the heart of the

Church during its best, most effective days, people like Saul of Tarsus and George Whitefield were introduced to God in a way that completely revolutionized their lives. He gave them beauty for ashes, the oil of joy for mourning, the garment of praise for the spirit of heaviness. He took these men from their world of black and white and transported them to a world of technicolor. They really began to live, not just exist. He gave them hope and a reason to live. They abandoned their old lives for new ones. That experience gave them a sense of identity. As they began growing in the Lord, it sharply defined some of the most practical aspects of Christianity, both in their personal lives and in their public ministries.

That first power encounter accomplished many things in their personal lives. It edified them, and it gave them peace and a realization of how brief this life is. It made them realize how big and awesome the Almighty God really is, while it also gave them joy because that same God sent His Son to die for them. You might say that their walks with God began with a bang. But this bang was all they knew. That was Christianity to them: an exciting experience with God. They knew no other kind of Christian life, so they assumed it should continue as it started. Therefore, they continued what had begun their spiritual lives: communication with God. They prayed, and every prayer they prayed was much like the first; it was a power encounter. Mortal, fallible man, interfaced with his immortal infallible Creator. Every day was not deliriously happy for them, but they had an inner peace. Those power encounters continually renewed their perspective and prevented them from being dragged off by the cares and distractions of this life. They were constantly reminded that knowing God is the purpose of life. Nothing else filled them with such hope, nor was anything greater or more desirable to them. Like all men, they sinned, but in accordance with the Scriptures, they found forgiveness and renewed fellowship with God. They often knew hardship, but they knew peace as well, despite their circumstances.

Their experience also heavily influenced their ministries. They weren't satisfied with just getting Christians to attend services, nor were they contented with just provoking a greater morality among the saints. Instead they wanted all believers to experience God like they did, experiencing the kind of life they were experiencing. What's more, they wanted the unchurched and the non-Christians to experience it as well. They wanted everyone's life to be totally wrapped up in God.

THE WAY THINGS ARE

Things have changed a lot since the last revival our nation saw. Many Christians today profess to be born again, but are unable to recall a specific moment when they turned their lives over to God. They don't recall having their lives dramatically transformed as the burden of their sin was released from them; or put another way, they didn't have a power encounter with Christ. I don't think this means they aren't saved. Generally the people who don't remember ever having a power encounter are people who have grown up in a good Bible-believing church. They went to Sunday school, learned the traditional Bible stories, and probably even heard the message of salvation all at a very young age. Generally, they grew up with Christian parents and every kind of Christian influence possible. Consequently when they were saved, very little changed for them. Their lives changed where eternity is concerned, but their lives on planet earth remained mostly the same, especially as children. They continued going to church, continued trying to obey the admonishments of the Scriptures, and so forth. For them, Christianity was a lifestyle, not a life of power encounters. Bear in mind these people are saved, but they have different ideas about what life is all about after salvation. Since they've never had a power encounter with God, they never seek one.

As a result, today's Church is staggering along, grossly

deficient in the area of experience with God. Many of these people, who have grown up in the church and now exercise much control in it, fear that experience with God will of necessity lead one to abandon the Scriptures as his guide. They believe that the power encounter is next of kin to chaos and that it will turn the church members into a rabble dependent on their shifting emotions rather than God's unchanging Word. Yet, I find very little historical basis for such fears, although such things could happen. Someone who has read the Bible could likewise abuse it as Jim Jones did. Yet, we don't abandon the Bible because it can be perverted by some. Similarly we cannot abandon experience with God simply because some can pervert it. In all the cases we have seen so far, experience with God has fostered a love for His Word and produced a more unshakable faith instead of acting as a detriment to either. No, such fears are irrational when taken to this extreme and barriers to all that God has in store for us.

God has more for us than we are seeing right now. The Church seems to be rather anemic. The Church's ministry is so inferior to what it has been in the past. A glance at the New Testament Church or at the early twentieth century revival bears this out. Today's believers are very heavily dependent on programs, systems, and certain prescribed methods for doing things. Clergy and laypeople alike are hunting for gimmickry strategies that they hope will assure successful evangelistic outreaches. Yet the fact is that the most successful outreaches and meetings that ever happened owed their success to something more than strategies concocted by mere men. Those great gatherings were so effective because of the power of the Holy Spirit in answer to prayer. Every one of the great revivals we examined was preceded by equally great prayer meetings. Yet we seem to have a prayerless Church that would rather ride in a horse-drawn wagon than fly in a supersonic jet—spiritually-speaking. The present-day Church almost seems to prefer inferiority.

However, the Church is neither dead nor dormant. I'm only saying Her deficiencies have placed it in a state of inferiority. People are getting saved daily. In many ways, they're like George Whitefield, walking a new path in life. But bear in mind that many (though by no means all) of the people who have been born and raised in the Church regard Christianity as a lifestyle. They, the majority, encourage new converts, the minority, to pursue a good Christian lifestyle. That is to say, they encourage them to witness, read the Bible, and practice what they read in the Bible. They try to encourage these babes in Christ to live lives holy and acceptable to God. There's nothing wrong with this. In fact that is exactly what they should be doing. What's wrong is they practice one good to the exclusion of another. They preach salvation, morality, and Christian responsibility to the exclusion of experience.

This has substantially weakened the Church. Christians (whom I might point out **are** the Church) frequently are saved, but fail to have a personal relationship with God. They may say they have one, but they are mistaken. They don't know what having a personal relationship with the Lord really is. They think it just means being saved. Saved people without a personal relationship with God invariably mean trouble, and that's exactly what we have.

I spoke to an Evangelical pastor recently about counseling couples planning to get married. He told me that he just assumes that they have already had sex by the time they approach him with the plans of their upcoming wedding. He was the pastor of a large church, considered to be very successful. I have heard similar remarks from other pastors. It's not a fluke. It's a piece of reality that's being carefully (and sometimes not so carefully) kept under wrap.

Marriages are in trouble in the Church. Go to almost any church of any denomination and you will likely see it infested with separations, divorces, and bitter couples. Believers who lack that fulfilling relationship with God are seeking fulfillment in marriage and are finding unhappiness instead. The Church is responding to this by formulating divorce recovery seminars and divorce recovery groups. We are committing the same error over and over: preaching one truth to the exclusion of another. While we are preaching the truth of God's love and forgiveness, we are neglecting to take a strong stand against divorce and are consequently creating a fertile environment in which more divorce can occur.

Meanwhile, other believers are becoming entangled in the cares of this world and are justifying it with Scripture. They point to the patriarchs and all of their wealth to justify their mad dash for money. An old proverb tells us Satan can quote Scripture to his own purpose. It seems that man shares this ability. And again, it is the same error: the practice of one truth to the exclusion of another. It is proclaimed that our unlimited God is our provider, but nothing is said about storing up riches for ourselves in heaven. Instead, an obsession with self-aggrandizement has resulted.

In addition, the saints are flocking to the movie theaters. When I make such a statement in this context, I am usually faced with unbelieving stares. Just about everyone wonders, "There's supposed to be something wrong with that?" Consider the fact that the stars of most every picture blaspheme God and break all His commandments (sometimes all in one motion picture). They fornicate, murder, lust, steal, commit adultery, envy, hate, **even to a sickening degree.** How can a born again saint of God be entertained by this? One individual responded to my question by saying, "It's not that you're entertained by those things." [I was already certain that I was not.] "You just ignore those things," he said, "and enjoy the movie."

Personally, I could not ignore those things and subsequently, could not enjoy the movie. But I said to him, "You can ignore sin? That's a reckless practice and reckless practices have a way of staying with you and spreading into other parts of life. It sounds at least as bad as being entertained by sin."

Blaise Pascall once correctly observed that there is a God-shaped vacuum inside every human being. However, I don't believe that being saved automatically fills that vacuum any more than I believe being saved means you have a relationship with the Lord. Just look at the last few paragraphs. Each illustrates a different way by which Christians are trying to fill that vacuum in their lives. Moreover, if that vacuum were filled in all believers' lives, we would not be in a state of crisis.

THE WAY THINGS WERE AND ARE IN MY LIFE

I know about that vacuum from experience. I sensed it was filled when I was saved, but as time went on, it seemed to resurface. I still remember feeling as a young pastor that something was missing in my life. I really didn't have the joy of my salvation anymore, and my ministry didn't seem to be very effective. I tried memorizing Scripture, but the words I memorized seemed to be little more than just that: words I had memorized. Then I tried reading more books by noted Christian authors, but that didn't seem to help either. Then I reasoned that what I needed was to continue my formal education, so my wife and I made plans to leave our home and church in St. Paul to move to Kenosha, Wisconsin so that I could attend a nearby seminary.

I was a bit distracted during those first days of classes. The church I had been attending was preparing for a prayer seminar taught by Dick Eastman, well-known for his ministry dealing exclusively with prayer. For some reason, I couldn't get my mind off it. When the first day of the seminar finally arrived, I found myself counting the hours until I could leave school to head for church. I wasn't sure what I expected, but I just sensed something was about to happen. And it did. I found what was missing in my life: **prayer.**

That prayer seminar was the beginning of an adventure with God. I found a new, deeper love for God than I had ever known before. My newly-acquired love and desire for God that I received through prayer drew me to pray even more. I even got to the point where I was skipping classes to go to the prayer room where I was spending hours on end. My relationship with the Lord grew deeper than I ever thought possible as I prayed, giving myself more and more to Him.

The effect prayer had on my life and ministry was equal to the effect salvation had. For several years, I had been searching for ways to be more effective for God. I had placed a great deal of hope in education, but my increased knowledge left me at the same distance from God with the same effectiveness I had before. Only when I began to pray and began to truly know God did I become more effective for God.

This doesn't mean that I'm opposed to higher education. I believe that an educated man who is sensitive to the Holy Spirit can be a great power force for God to use. The learned Saul of Tarsus was an excellent example of this. However, we mustn't rely on higher education to do things it was never intended to do. God was calling me to a life and ministry of prayer, and all the education in the world could not develop it.

I was a Christian, saved by Christ's atoning work on the Cross. In many ways, God was not a real part of my life, or simply put another way, I didn't have a relationship with Him. I had all the Christian things, but not a relationship with Christ. We have a relationship with Christ in our lives only to the extent that we pray. We can read the Bible from cover to cover, but still not have a relationship with Him. It's just like being able to read a book by the prime minister of France. We may gain insight into the French prime minister by reading the book, but we'll never really get a sense of knowing the man just by reading about him.

It may sound simplistic, but God is the solution to our

crisis. We can reach Him only by means of prayer. Our pastors and churches must get back to prayer and the close relationship with God it produces or face spiritual stagnation. It is in prayer that we can rediscover the power encounter, and in many ways, rediscover our God. It was just simple people like you and me praying that led to the great revivals of the past. It may sound too easy, but then getting saved also sounded too easy to most of us. Yet, there is a complex side to all of this that we will see in the next chapter as we examine the process whereby a revival dies its slow death.

CHAPTER THREE
CISTERNS THAT HOLD NO WATER

> "I am rich; I have acquired wealth and do not need a thing."
> —Church of Laodicea, A.D. 96

It was an era in which people only dreamed of television, and only the most imaginative did that. It was an era that neither witnessed nor heard of world wars, to say nothing of nuclear weapons capable of devastating the surface of the entire planet. It was a world during which old-timers waited for that "horseless buggy fad" to come to the halt they predicted. Yet, it was in this "primitive" society of the early 1900s that an evangelist named Gladys Pearson preached a startling warning, a warning which spelled out an eventual decline and decay for a revival that spread around the globe and spanned several Protestant denominations.

It is a warning that has gone unheeded through the decades, and one which, if unheeded, will serve as an epitaph for this generation of believers in the near future. It is this fearsome warning that will act as the basis for this chapter in an effort to clearly explain why the Church is in such grave trouble and why that revival and all the others that preceded it subsided.

THE PATRIARCHAL PARALLEL

"When Abram was ninety-nine years old, the Lord appeared to him and said, 'I am God Almighty; walk before me and be blameless. I will confirm my covenant between me and you and will greatly increase your numbers.' Abram fell facedown, and God said to him, 'As for me, this is my covenant with you: You will be the father of many nations. No longer will you be called Abram; your name will be Abraham, for I have made you a father of many nations'" (Gen. 17:1-5).

It was during the generation of Abraham that God began to do something new. Abraham was in the first generation of this new covenant relationship with God. Abraham could be likened to those early believers who met at the Upper Room in Jerusalem or likened to those who gathered at the first camp meetings. They, too, were the first generation to experience something new that God was doing. Their parents had never seen the likes of it, nor had their grandparents. They were pioneers, just as Abraham was.

By studying Abraham, we can see certain characteristics that are shared universally by first-generation believers. They are characteristics common to all such believers regardless of comparative cultural or technological variations. The chief thing we notice about Abraham is that he was an altar-builder. He almost couldn't make it through a single chapter in Genesis without building an altar. This shouldn't be viewed as some sort of architectural zeal which consumed

Abraham. It has much more spiritual significance than that.

Altar-building is symbolic of prayer, or perhaps we could say that prayer is symbolic of building. In either case, there is a direct relationship. Abraham built the numerous altars he built so that he could worship God and sacrifice to Him. Wasn't he building altars to accomplish the same ends we are when we pray? Of course he was. Although we do not need sacrifices to atone for our sins (we already have One), we offer sacrifices: we pray.

So, we can safely say that Abraham possessed the spirit of a prayer warrior, manifesting that spirit everywhere he went as he built altar after altar to sacrifice to God. This urgency and zeal after prayer is business-as-usual for first-generation believers like Abraham. These believers are establishing a new movement and are constantly on the offensive, blazing a trail for their descendants.

Abraham had one other very noticeable liking: digging wells. If Abraham went through an entire chapter of Genesis without building an altar, then he dug a well instead. As was the case earlier, Abraham's actions did not reflect a love for construction work. His wells were a reflection of his desire to bless others. Any one of those wells would have indeed been a blessing for someone on one of those sweltering days the Middle East is known for. Those wells also symbolized a great deal of hard work and self-denial (if you've ever dug a well, you know what I mean).

Unfortunately, both of these traits began to fade in the subsequent generations. His descendants didn't follow his example, but instead indulged themselves in luxury in the land God gave to their father, who was a millionaire in his day because of the Lord's kindness to him.

For the first generation of any movement, the prayer and self-sacrifice Abraham practiced with such fervor are a must. They must pray, and pray, and pray, and pray. They have no blessings initially. The only thing they can offer God at the altar is themselves. But as time marches on, and as God is faithful, blessings come to them as surely as they came for Abraham. Then, like Abraham, they begin to dig wells of blessings for their children as their churches become more organized and better equipped. But the second generation walks in next, and that's when the trouble starts.

THE SPIRITUAL GENERATION GAP

In the patriarchal case we've been studying, Isaac was the second generation. Because his father, Abraham, was a man who diligently sought after God, Isaac was the recipient of fabulous blessings. His father, a well-digger of the first order, had invested his life establishing something for Isaac to move into, freeing him from the weighty burden of starting from scratch.

However, this freedom is not without its drawbacks. For instance, the second generation doesn't place the same priority on "altar-building" and "well-digging" that the first generation did. The ideas of sacrifice and self-denial are not a must for them. Similarly, prayer is not held in the high esteem that it was a generation before. This is due, at least in part, to the comfortable setting they've stepped into. There's no struggling to build a church in their case. Everything is pretty much downhill; at least for them it is. But their children will not receive the same blessings because we cannot establish substantial blessings for the next generation without prayer.

It is without prayer that the second generation tries to improve upon what the first generation accomplished. When prayerless Isaac did this, he ran into trouble: "Isaac's servants dug in the valley and discovered a well of fresh water there. But the herdsman of Gerar quarreled with Isaac's herdsmen and said, 'The water is ours!' So he named the well Esek [dispute, strife], because they disputed with him. Then they dug another well, but they quarreled over that one also; so he named it Sitnah [opposition, envy]" (Gen. 26:19-21).

This is a textbook case of man without prayer trying to

improve upon a plan God established in a people of prayer. Isaac, not a prayer warrior like his father, tried to improve upon his dad's work and collided with envy and strife, very human problems.

Yet, there is more to this story, for just a verse earlier, in Genesis 26:18, we are informed that "Isaac reopened the wells that had been dug in the time of his father Abraham..." That was where Isaac found the blessings. Earlier, when he dug new wells, he received only envy and strife. It was then that Isaac did something different, something most second generations don't do: he realized that his father's ways were the only ways that worked. He went back to his father's wells. Unfortunately, most second generation believers don't do this. Most forge on ahead, trying to improve upon—**without** prayer—what was established **in** prayer. That which was a must for the first generation becomes a convenience for the second generation.

This is not really a case of evil rebellion. These subsequent believers are not fighting against what their parents began. It's just that their spiritual circumstances are nothing like what their parents' were. It's difficult for these young people who have received so many blessings to grasp what their parents went through. They were never victims of egg-hurling scorners, as their parents were. They can't relate to that. Neither can they relate to having nothing—no beautiful church building, no dignified reputation, etc., but having only God. No, because of the blessings they have received, they do not face the same circumstances which helped to shape their parents' faith. It's because they don't really understand what their elders held most important that they try to improve upon things.

I recall speaking to a pastor (a second-generation Christian) who confirmed this suspicion of mine. When he grew up, family camp was **the** place to go. Everyone who was anyone in the church went to family camp. However, family camp was an experience he came to dread because of his ultra-strict father who forbade him from even moving his eyes from the platform. If his father caught him so much as glancing at one of the other children in the building, it meant a spanking. As a result of this, when he became a father he never steered his children toward family camp for fear that the slightest coaxing might recreate his own childhood problem for his children.

Of course, I'd have to say that this pastor's father was quite extreme in his disciplinary measures, but this story is not meant to be an illustration in child-rearing. The point of the story is that the older man was adamant in the extreme about something, and his son was never able to understand why. This is very typical of first generation-second generation relations. The first generation becomes ardent about certain things because they paid a great price to found and establish the movement that is entrusted to bring these things to the Church and to the world.

The problem with this elder group is that they assume that their descendants will automatically understand why they feel as strongly as they do about certain issues, but their children will never just automatically know. They can't. Their world and the spiritual environment in which they grew up is so different that they can't just somehow end up walking the same path. Sadly enough, though, because the first generation assumes they understand, they never take the time to explain it to their children, and from here, the problem snowballs. It is important to understand that the second generation never forgets what was important to Mom and Dad; they simply don't understand why it was important.

THE SCHEMERS

The result is a movement which has changed in all but name from what it was at its inception. By the third generation, we have believers who can't understand in the slightest the convictions of their elders. By this time, what was a must for the first generation and a convenience for the second, becomes nonsense to the third.

All this talk about doing things the old way makes no sense to the average third-generation believer. The old ways, it is said, are for the old days, and the new days require new ways. The third-generation believers claim that in this area, we are dealing with cultural issues when we are not. Prayer is no cultural issue. It transcends all cultures, societies, and ages. It should be basic to every generation everywhere.

In addition, the third generation becomes a group of schemers, like Jacob, their equivalent in Genesis. It is hard for us to think of ourselves as schemers and connivers. However, look at how we have developed an approach to God that shows us to be exactly that. We act like little children who have discovered a secret. We take God's promises and demand that God honor them. We fuse different verses together with a smug attitude that we have God over a barrel; He must come through. We even scheme to cover a lack of holiness under the guise of cultural differences, personal tastes, and individual backgrounds. Like Jacob, we have become deceivers and supplanters. We are always scouting out new ways, while ignoring the old way, the way of prayer.

Anyone who went to Sunday school as a child knows the story about how Jacob conned his brother Esau into giving him his birthright. Shortly after that, Jacob's mother heard Esau say that he wanted to kill Jacob. It was something everyone—including Jacob—took seriously, for it was then that his mother sent him away to marry one of Laban's daughters. In Genesis 32, some years later, Jacob was about to come face to face with not just his brother, but also with his own deceit. Jacob had left Laban and was crossing the desert when he got word that Esau and four hundred of his men were coming toward him.

At this point Jacob was fearing for his life. He doubted that his chicanery had slipped Esau's mind over the years (It's funny how things like that stick in people's minds, isn't it?). He had to do something. As was natural for him, he did things his way instead of God's way. He tried to buy his brother off, or to put it more delicately in his own words, "...I will pacify him with these [special] gifts..." (Gen. 32:20). This is par for the course for the third-generation believer. For him, money becomes his god. It is looked upon as the cure-all. It is important to the conniver to have a tool with which to do his dirty work. He finds money to be the perfect implement. (Of course, to keep things spiritual, he must reaffirm that it is God who supplies his monetary "fix." Greed and materialism are then elevated to the status of theology.)

"So Jacob's gifts went on ahead of him, but he himself spent the night in the camp. That night Jacob got up and took his two wives, his two maidservants and his eleven sons and crossed the ford of the Jabbok. After he had sent them across the stream, he sent over all his possessions. So Jacob was left alone, and a man wrestled with him till daybreak" (Gen. 32:21-24).

I believe the phrase "Jacob was left alone" is significant. There was nobody else around, no one to talk to, and nothing in particular to do. Most importantly, there was no one else to blame his problems on (which is typical of a conniver). When we are left alone to face God, we are left with no choice but to confront ourselves for who we really are. For Jacob, as for many of us, it was no easy task. The Book of Genesis tells us that an angel wrestled with Jacob all night. I'm sure that Jacob was not just wrestling with an angel that night. He was also wrestling with himself. He looked deep inside himself and realized who and what he really was. He didn't like what he saw about himself and wanted to change.

Consequently, he would not let go of the angel for fear that he would come out of the ordeal the same old Jacob. He was determined not to let the angel go until that angel had blessed him. Interestingly enough, the angel asked, "What is your name?" I often wondered why the angel would ask such a question. The angel was dealing with this man who wanted to be blessed, didn't like himself the way he was. And so, the angel asks what his name is. What did Jacob's name have to do with anything? Finally, it struck me that the angel was trying to get Jacob to admit who he really was. When Jacob humbled himself and admitted, "I am Jacob," it was humbling because Jacob's name was synonymous with "supplanter," or more colloquially, "conniver." Then the angel replied, "Your name shall no longer be Jacob, but Israel." At that point, Jacob was a new man.

What changed Jacob was admitting who and what he was. It was a moment of admittance and repentance, and it was his own decision to return to the wells of his grandfather, Abraham. After this, he knew true blessings from above, from the Father of heavenly lights, from the Lord of love. These blessings were already established, but he could not receive them until he admitted the error of his ways and returned to the old, true ways.

The results of Jacob's transformation were really quite amazing. To begin with, he no longer feared his brother because when our relationship with God is right, we do not fear men. Besides that, his brother forgave him and ceased carrying a grudge. It was a fulfillment of a proverb a man named Solomon would write centuries later: "When a man's ways are pleasing to the Lord, he makes even his enemies to live at peace with him" (Prov. 16:7).

The story concludes by telling how Esau ran to meet Jacob and embraced him, throwing his arms around his neck and kissing him as they wept together. What a reunion! Unfortunately, it is a very singular one because so few will humble themselves as Jacob did to return to the old way of prayer.

BROKEN CISTERNS

The prophet Jeremiah quoted the Lord as saying, "My people have committed two sins: They have forsaken me, the spring of living water, and have dug their own cisterns, broken cisterns that cannot hold water" (Jer. 2:13). This same problem arises time after time throughout the history of God's dealings with man. It has happened from the time of the patriarchs to this very day. God's people wander away from Him and His ways and concoct their own plans and strategies based on man's limited perception of reality. They do things their way, not caring to so much as utter a word to God about it to seek His advice.

Jeremiah clarified the problem by saying in verse 32, "Does a maiden forget her jewelry, a bride her wedding ornaments? Yet my people have forgotten me, days without number." These comparisons were being used to make God's people see how absurd it was for them to cease seeking after God in all their doings. For one of God's people to quit seeking Him wholeheartedly would be like a bride's marching down the aisle to "Here Comes the Bride" without her wedding gown. It would be like a woman of meager means nonchalantly casting her few pieces of fine jewelry down a wishing well. Such scenarios simply aren't natural. They're strange and bizarre—almost as much so as the people of God not praying and pursuing God with all their heart. Such a people cut themselves off from the Spring of Living Water and subsequently have nothing to fill their cisterns with. What is left is an empty shell, merely an empty hull of theology.

In many areas of the Church which were experiencing revival less than a century ago, that's all that is left. See for yourself how often we talk about peace and yet are afraid of the future. We talk about the strength of the Lord, yet more Christian marriages are breaking up than ever before. If we do not purpose in our hearts to seek God with all of our being, this will become our status quo. We will have nothing to offer people besides empty theology, little more than a weak religious philosophy.

Any people guilty of this first sin (i.e., forsaking Him, the Spring of Living Water) will also be guilty of the second one Jeremiah mentioned: digging their own cisterns, broken cisterns that cannot hold water. That is to say that since they have quit seeking God, the Spring of Living Water, their wells are empty. Not only is there no water to fill them with, but they are fractured wells, marred by human problems. The well represents the work of God. The work of God is to prepare blessings for the next generation. The water represents God. Water is life; without it, nothing lives.

Without prayer, not only is the work of God full of holes and fractures, but we don't end up with enough of God to fill the well. Christianity is reduced to a litany of religious activities. We may have our theology polished and finely tuned, but we have nothing from experience to hand down to our children.

By and large, the Church has rejected prayer and seeking God as a viable, realistic, practical solution to the problems of life. Instead of seeking God, we're contriving our own inferior game plans. Since we don't really believe in God's faithfulness in response to prayer, we no longer visit those in need with the hopes of truly ministering to them in Jesus' name. When the needy reach into an empty well, all they grasp at is air because there is no substance.

Christians did not always run around looking diligently for ways to minister to people without prayer. It was exactly the opposite in the early days of the Church and in the days of revival. At those times, saints realized that God has complete, total, and unlimited power. This being the case, it was only logical to seek the solution to any given problem in God. That's why their ministry was so successful.

For example, one man named John Hyde, a former missionary to India, habitually invested his best time in prayer. It was in prayer that he sensed God placing a challenge before him to win one soul every day. One year later, he had personally led over four hundred people to Jesus. He then felt prompted to win two people to Christ each day. Please note that if he failed to touch that number of people, he went back to the prayer closet, not to the local

Christian bookstore to find yet another gimmickry evangelism outline. Please also note, that the thrust of Hyde's life was not witnessing. He lived for a higher, more noble purpose: to draw ever closer to Him by whom he was eternally saved. In fact, he drew so close to Christ that the Jesus in him simply drew people to the River of Life. Evangelism was not an end in and of itself. It was simply the result of a life of prayer with an undivided heart.

John Hyde approached ministry by emulating Christ. He held Jesus up as his hero and prime example. There was no one he tried more to imitate. He did his best to pray like Christ, and as a result of that time invested in prayer, he became even more and more like Christ. His philosophy of ministry was, "I must look like Christ in order to attract sinners." A prayerless church has adopted a totally different philosophy. Today our approach to ministry is to look like the world. We are convinced that the only way to reach the world is to look like the world. The only way to reach Satanists is to look like Satan. What more could we expect from a Church that spends so little time in God's presence? The unhappy result is that Christians today can hardly be distinguished from non-Christians. Moreover, the world sees little hope for them in us. I learned this lesson the hard way during a hospital call I made on behalf of my church.

At the hospital, I spoke to a teenage girl who had attempted suicide. Upon noticing that every square inch of space was obscured by rock music posters, I recalled that the church was having a "Christian" rock concert and decided to invite the girl. Then the Holy Spirit spoke to my heart saying, "You would offer her an imitation of the world and its things, the same things that led her to attempt suicide?"

I believe the world is looking for something different. However, if we do not become again a people who zealously go after God, we will never have that something different to offer them. Psychologists will be able to offer them as much as we are, and we will be left alone and confused with a stale religion which offers neither the power to change men's lives nor the strength to maintain our own lagging momentum. We will dig empty wells which produce empty relationships with Christ.

THE KEY GENERATION

What I have described thus far is a cycle. It is a pattern of events which repeats itself at regular intervals. Importantly, it is a cycle which only lasts three generations, meaning that at the end of the third generation, it can be expected to start all over again with a new move of God out of which a new denomination may or may not spring. This makes the first and third generations the key generations. I believe this is why Abram (first generation) and Jacob (third generation) had their names changed, whereas Isaac (second generation) did not.

If we examine Abram carefully, we will see that he needed a drastic change in his life. God needed to do some work on him before this man would be able to be the earthly head of a brand new plan of God. He needed to be a man of power and strength. He needed a power encounter with God to bring this about, and he had it. Then, symbolic of a new beginning and a new destiny as "the father of many nations," God changed his name to "Abraham."

Isaac, on the other hand, had no real need to change. He grew up in the midst of a revival of sorts. He had all the blessings. He had it "made in the shade." All he had to do was sustain the revival through prayer, but he failed to do this.

It is because Isaac failed to sustain the revival through prayer that his descendant, Jacob, was in need of a power encounter since the revival died. Therefore, the third generation becomes most crucial because it is these people who will usher in the next generation, the generation which will begin the cycle all over again with a revival. Today, there are those who know they need a power encounter, just as Jacob did. These people are calling for a return to the basics and the roots of Christianity. However, at the same time, there is a group which is seeking new ways, relying on new methods and new technology to carry out the work of the Church. One thing is certain: the faction which repents of its deception and stops trying to do things its own way will be the one to usher in a revival.

Repentance is as necessary for us as it was for Jacob. But like him, we won't come to it easily. Consider the PTL scandal that rocked the Church world back in 1987. That was an exposure of the corruption that unfortunately exists within popular Evangelical Christianity. Just about every born again believer who had taken a stand for Christ had to deal with the scorn of unbelievers. Yet, did it bring us to our knees? Not at all. We said, "Jim Bakker is the guilty one. He is the deceiver. He needs to repent." The only thing unique about Jim Bakker is that he practiced what was in his heart. Does that make him worse than those who have not practiced what was in their heart just the same? Jesus said that to think it was to do it. On this basis, which of us has a right to cast a stone at Jim Bakker? Jim Bakker was symptomatic of our era's Christianity, and it will take more than the repentance of that one man to alleviate our crisis.

Why weren't American Evangelicals broken over the sin that was discovered in their own ranks? It is because we couldn't believe that we are the supplanter, that we need to repent and draw closer to our God. Almost no one believed that Jim Bakker was anything but an exception to the rule, but I believe he was a very average specimen, unique only because he practiced what his heart was full of—and was caught.

There remains in this issue one last significant factor for us to consider: Joseph (a type of Christ), the fourth generation, the generation of revival. Where do you believe we stand in history? I believe we stand in the midst of a third generation that God wants to use to help usher in the second coming of Jesus Christ. When I was saved in 1973, there was much talk about the return of Christ. There was much activity in Israel. The Seven-Day War had concluded five years earlier, and most Christians were consumed with the thought that if we could diligently do the work of God, spreading the gospel to the four corners of the earth, we could actually affect the return of Christ. Today, however, the mentality seems to be, "I wish Jesus would get here soon. Things here are really bad." I believe God wants us to shake the dust from our feet and get back to concerning ourselves with taking this message of salvation to our neighbors and the world. That would build our dependency on prayer once again.

HOPE

There is certainly hope for the second and third-generation Christians. With God, there is always hope. If it were not so, I would greatly fear for my son, who will be a second-generation Christian. However, he's not doomed to be a wishy-washy Christian just because he won't meet Christ as powerfully as I did. He has the potential to be a Christian walking very closely with God. How? I must teach him that he can have regular power encounters with God through prayer.

As I said earlier, second and third-generation Christians are at a disadvantage because they don't have the same motivation to pray as their forefathers who experienced revival. But that doesn't mean they can't or won't pray. All it means is that they need the instruction of a first-generation believer. This means that my son, for example, needs me to provide the motivation and instruction to get him started in a life centered on communicating with and experiencing his Heavenly Father.

WILL WE RESPOND?

On June 22, 1941, Germany invaded the USSR in spite of the nonaggression pact the two countries had signed only a few years earlier. The Nazis met very little opposition and were even welcomed as liberators from Joseph Stalin's tyranny. When Joseph Stalin received word of the invasion, he offered very little comment other than his assurance that he had signed a pact with Hitler guaranteeing peace between them. Still, men continued pouring into his office trying to convince him that they were being invaded by Germany. Stalin's impatience turned to outright fury, and he declared that the next idiot who dared disturb him with the nonsense about a German invasion would be shot. Richard Sorge, a Soviet spy who had infiltrated the Nazi party and received an ambassadorial post in the German embassy in Japan, radioed word to Stalin that the Germans were indeed invading the USSR—and were doing so with great success. Stalin replied with a terse order of silence flanked by a very serious threat if any further warning about Germany were sent...Then he took off for a two-week vacation to his villa, leaving instructions that anyone who tried to disturb him would be shot. More than a week passed before Stalin and his Politburo determined a response to the invasion. But by that time, most of European Russia had fallen to the Nazis. In fact, Stalin's failure to act allowed the Germans to advance to within fifteen miles of Moscow.

Like that vicious dictator of many years ago, we too, have a decision to make. How will we respond to the warnings that we are hearing? Before we criticize Stalin for his response to the Nazi threat, perhaps we should first analyze our own response to the threat which faces the Church. Many reports are coming in which warn us of a threat. Will we be like Stalin, so arrogant that we won't consider the possibility that anything can really threaten us? As indicators of danger are flashing all around us, are we planning on taking a vacation? Or will we put on the full armor of God and prepare for battle, a battle we must wage on our knees?

CHAPTER FOUR

TODAY'S CHURCH: LIMITED TO MAN'S ABILITIES

> "The church that is man-managed instead of God-governed is doomed to failure. A ministry that is college-trained, but not Spirit-filled works no miracles."
> —Samuel Chadwick

Sometimes warnings are unpopular but necessary all the same. Throughout man's history, many great disasters have been the result of silence. Insightful people have perceived danger, but have decided to keep it to themselves because their warning cries would have been unpopular. The Second World War is a case in point. During the years between Adolf Hitler's rise to power and the outbreak of World War II, most European politicians kept their suspicions about the German military build up to themselves and just told their constituents exactly what they wanted to hear:

there would not be another world war.

No one was more guilty of this than Stanley Baldwin, British prime minister during the early 1930s when Hitler came to power and began rearming Germany. Baldwin was aware of the pacifistic sentiments which had taken hold of the minds and hearts of the British populace since the settlement of "the Great War," as it was called. World War I had robbed the nation of nearly an entire generation of young men. Hardly a family was left in Britain that was not scarred by the death of a loved one killed in a war the purpose of which no one really understood. Knowing this, Baldwin, a slick politician, assured the public that the Germans, who had been too severely punished at the conclusion of World War I, were simply developing defensive capabilities that they had been unjustly denied by the terms of the Treaty of Versailles which officially ended hostilities between Germany and the Allied and Associated powers. He knew that the people would elect only a leader who would ease their fears and guarantee them that there was not going to be another devastating war. He knew Winston Churchill was out of power, cooling his heels in outermost recesses of the Parliament building because he had been branded an eccentric war-monger: he warned that another great war was inevitable if men like the Nazis were allowed to develop formidable military capabilities.

Today's Christians are much like the majority of British people were in the 1930s. They just want to be assured that everything is all right, and there are many modern-day Stanley Baldwins who are doing just that. They are preachers who are promising the Church that everything is fine; all we need to do is claim the promises of the Scriptures and we will be barraged by prosperity and success. I wish that were true, but it is not. The Baldwins of the Church are correct in that we need to claim the promises of God's Word, but they fail to recognize the unfortunate state of God's Church in the West. In this chapter, we will look more closely at the Church, not in revival, lacking the blessings of revival, and working feverishly to compensate for those missing blessings.

WANTED: A REPLACEMENT FOR THE HOLY SPIRIT

As the flames of the revival from the early 1900s have been extinguished, the Church has become increasingly less effective. Just review chapter one of this book and consider how often you have seen such phenomenal results in your church. Faced with halfhearted saints and minimal church growth, our clergy has begun to search for some kind of remedy to this spiritual malady. Most pastors would like to find something that would draw out multitudes of saints and sinners alike as the first camp meetings did, and I'm sure they'd love to see their congregations as head-over-heels in love with God as those old believers were. I believe that since we are looking for the kind of results revival brings, we should do the kinds of things people did that brought revival: hold solemn assemblies, pray, fast, and diligently seek our God. That is when God responds and the Holy Spirit moves out and accomplishes what no human being can do by himself. However, that can take years of faithfulness in prayer but we are in a prayerless Church, and since God sends His Holy Spirit only in response to prayer, it seems like the Holy Spirit is ruled out.

What we have finally accepted to help us out is our own giftedness. We seem to rely excessively on our own strategies, our own ingenuity, on our God-given talents, and on the technology the last century has spawned. The latter item is particularly interesting because it seems to lead us to the others. Our era's technology has enabled us to reach more people at one time than ever before in the history of the world. This is exciting, but it seems that this excitement has clouded our perspective for improving our techniques for spreading the good news.

FOR SALE (CHEAP!): THE FRUIT OF THE SPIRIT

This tendency to regard professionalism and perfectionism above the Holy Spirit is less obvious among lay people than among some of the "celebrity clergy" who produce our Christian mass media. Christian talk shows must use trendy graphics, feature beautiful sets, and prove as entertaining as the Phil Donahue or Oprah Winfrey shows. If they don't compare favorably in those categories, many believers consider them failures. Similarly, TV preachers must feature the same professional graphics and camera work and prove as entertaining as a secular celebrity or their credibility is damaged. And, of course, Christian musicians must follow all the trends that secular musicians do to placate a large number of Christians. Their clothes, hairstyles, album covers, and music style must mirror the fads of the world or else they, too, are thought ill of. But it doesn't stop with Christians in the national spotlight. Local pastors soon get judged by the same standards as does the ministry of his church.

At one time, the fruit of the Holy Spirit established the credibility of a minister of the gospel. If someone was visiting a church for the first time, he would determine the pastor's legitimacy by asking questions like: "Does this man have love? Does he have joy? Does he have self-control?" If he didn't, he was no man of God because the absence of the fruit of the Spirit in his life was a sure indicator that he was spending a woefully inadequate amount of time in prayer. And who would want a pastor who didn't spend great amounts of time in prayer? If, on the other hand, a man exemplified the fruit of the Spirit, people accepted his ministry because it was obvious that he was a praying pastor, and **that's** the kind of pastor a believer wanted. Most personal accounts about the life of John Wesley glow with testimonies to his joy and his love and concern for people. In days gone by, believers wanted that anointing of God on a preacher's life, something only a closeness to God could bring.

Today, however, anyone can **buy** the anointing. It's called "air time." Any pastor, evangelist, or preacher who can afford to pay the monetary price can become an anointed man of God (or so we think) provided his presentation can match the secular world's. Consequently, anything anybody says on Christian television or radio is considered straight from God.

The anointing was not such a marketable commodity in the New Testament: "When Simon saw that the Spirit was given at the laying on of the apostles' hands, he offered them money and said, 'Give me this ability so that everyone on whom I lay my hands may receive the Holy Spirit.' Peter answered him: 'May your money perish with you, because you thought you could buy the gift of God with money! You have no part or share in this ministry, because your heart is not right before God'" (Acts 8:18-21).

Revivals tend to begin with a powerful wave of the Holy Spirit. Because of the Holy Spirit, they also begin with powerful men of God who respond to Simon much as Peter did. Today, unfortunately, we are left with many preachers who are much more like Simon than they are like the apostle. It is very desirable today to have the masses think that the touch of God is on your life and ministry. But it is not desirable to invest time in God's presence to receive that divine touch. It is not only more fashionable, but also easier, to depend upon creativity, showmanship, and personality instead of the Holy Spirit.

Paul was diametrically opposed to parading one's own ability in lieu of the Holy Spirit. Perhaps you will recall the following words of Paul: "When I came to you, brothers, I did not come with eloquence or superior wisdom as I proclaimed to you the testimony about God. For I resolved to know nothing while I was with you except Jesus Christ and him crucified. I came to you in weakness and fear, and with much trembling. My message and my preaching were not with wise and persuasive words, but with a demonstration of the Spirit's power" (1 Cor. 2:1-4).

Today our message is in evidence of showmanship and state of the art technology. Paul, on the other hand, was convinced that the Holy Spirit would confirm his words. But we ask, "Can the Holy Spirit confirm our word of strong families with drug-free teens and stable marriages?"

A.W. Tozer once said, "The Great Commission is not the first call to the Church." Such a statement shocks many whose lives are consumed with fine tuning their churches to draw in new members, but I must agree with Tozer. He reminds us that Jesus first told his disciples to go to Jerusalem and tarry there until they were endued with power from on high. Tozer concludes that Jesus had no desire for them to do the work of God until they had a power encounter with Him.

The disciples were very much like Christians who have grown up in the church. The disciples had already been living with Jesus for the past three years. Christianity was already a way of life for them. Jesus realized that they needed a power encounter before they could carry out the work God had for them.

"DO I NOW PLEASE GOD, OR MAN?"

Today's church has developed what I term **efficiency**, a philosophy overstating the importance of doing things right. Under this philosophy, every Evangelical church should be constructed "right." It should be the most opulent place of worship in town, featuring state of the art sound systems, the latest in stain guard carpeting, and the best padded pews. It must be an architectural marvel. Similarly, the ministry of that church must resemble the best the world has to offer in terms of external things. Each individual involved must rival the latest secular entertainer.

The rallying cry of the Church has become, "Come on! Let's do it right! We'll prove to that evil world that we can put on a show every bit as good as theirs." In its mad dash to employ twentieth-century technology to further the cause of Christ, the Church has become consumed with emulating the style and showmanship that accompanies this technology in the secular world. The secular media has attempted to be as crowd-pleasing as possible, and the Church has followed their lead. The soothing, entertaining services that result are seldom offensive, so they frequently draw people to the church organization.

On the other hand, the Holy Spirit is **effective**. While efficiency strives to do things right, effectiveness strives to do right things. Right things are those which concern God most. God is concerned most about doing what needs to be done to deliver unsaved people from the wages of their sins. That means we cannot compromise and may even—oh, no! Not that!—offend some people.

Efficiency leads us to do the work of God in the most inoffensive way, which often results in compromise. No one is going to be offended by one of our services, no sir! Why, that might impede the numerical growth of the church. Instead, we can now present all that the Bible says in such a way that every visitor will find the church to be a fun, comfortable place to be because it does things right.

If all we are drawing people to is an organization, then the organization must continually change (i.e., compromise) to keep everybody happy. Strong standards must come down because the morals of this world are coming down.

MORAL-SETTERS OR TREND-SETTERS?

God never called the Church to be a trend-setter. The Church should instead be a moral-setter. However, today instead of our effecting the trends of the world by maintaining high standards, these same trends are dictating our standards. If you're intent on being an "in" Christian, you wouldn't be caught dead in anything but the latest "designer" fashions.

I'm not against nice clothes, but I am adamantly opposed to fashion that countermands our morals. I remember talking to an ex-prostitute in a church who excitedly told me about all the things God had been teaching her since she was saved. To my initial surprise, one of the things she was learning about was fashion. She said that the Lord was teaching her what clothing she, as His child, should wear. I couldn't help asking what she thought about the fashion statement the Church was making. "I see 'Christian' women dressed like prostitutes all too often," she replied. "I see women in the Church wearing clothes designed to arouse men, clothes that the Holy Spirit has told me never to wear again now that I represent Jesus Christ."

I'm sure many of you remember when the mini-skirt was popular in the late 1960s and early 1970s. Do you know when that fashion ceased to be "in" with teenage girls? The mini skirt went "out" when mothers began wearing them. When I was in high school mini-skirts weren't the only fad. There was also a more dangerous fad: marijuana. Do you know when teens began using more powerful drugs? It was when Dad began smoking joints. When the moral-setters lower their standards, their moral subordinates lower their standards even more.

This is especially true when we consider the Church of Jesus Christ. We, the Church, are supposed to be the number one moral-setters on this planet. When we lower our standards, the world drops its standards also, becoming even worse. Because the Church is continually lowering Her standards, She is now faced with problems that should not arise in God's house.

A HOUSE OF PRAYER?

Whenever the Church lacks discernment, She has a problem recognizing sin for what it is. We are dealing more with marriage counseling today more than ever before. Why? We say that it is simply because there are more marriages falling apart today. But why are they falling apart? I think they're falling apart because we are afraid to preach on the sin of divorce for fear of offending the many divorced and remarried people in our churches.

"Then he entered the temple area and began driving out those who were selling. 'It is written,' he said to them, "'My house will be a house of prayer"; but you have made it "a den of robbers"''" (Luke 19;45,46). In verse 46, Jesus was making prayer preeminent. He was saying that prayer should stand out above all other things in the house of God. If prayer is not first and foremost, we lose our discernment as I described above. Jesus went on to say that when those in God's house don't pray, they rob God. It becomes a den of thieves.

Mindful of how the money-changers in the temple were "evicted" by Jesus, we in Christianity have sought (unsuccessfully) to keep money-changers out of the Church. However, there was nothing wrong with the money-changers being there. The problem with them was that they had become thieves. Yet, that was not the greatest problem. The greatest problem was that they had become thieves and **nobody** noticed! They didn't notice because they had lost their discernment, and they had lost their discernment because they were not praying. Jesus was really getting to the root of their problem when He highlighted the point that God's house is to be, first of all, a house of prayer.

The lack of discernment has never been more evident than it is today. Why else would the national news media need to call attention to the sins of the Church as it did in 1987 with all the televangelist scandals? Shouldn't the Church see these things before the world does? Another thing that really concerns me is that when the Church does see these things first, it is frequently the non-clergy who sees them before the clergy. Why does it take a national scandal to cause us to take action? It is because our prayerlessness has blinded us to our own sins.

Wouldn't it be wonderful for pastors to realize that the Church can raise the morals of the world by maintaining Her own high standards?

IN THE NEW TESTAMENT

"After we had been there a number of days, a prophet named Agabus came down from Judea. Coming over to us, he took Paul's belt, tied his own hands and feet with it and said, 'The Holy Spirit says, "In this way the Jews of Jerusalem will bind the owner of this belt and will hand him over to the Gentiles"'" (Acts 21:10-11).

Paul was warned that he would be severely persecuted during his upcoming trip to Jerusalem, but he went anyway and was persecuted just as Agabus had prophesied. Just as a mob of enraged Jews were beating him, Paul was rescued and arrested by a group of Roman soldiers and officers intent on quieting the uproar. Shortly after, Paul was allowed to defend himself in front of all the people. It was a perfect opportunity for him to present the gospel in a "less offensive" way. A small compromise, a few ambiguous phrases, and some carefully chosen words could have made Paul the most popular fellow in town.

However, Paul chose another course of action. In Acts, chapter 22, he told the crowd about his power encounter with Christ. He did this because he wanted the people to find Christ in the same dynamic way he did (the only way to find Christ, as far as Paul was concerned). This didn't gain any popularity for him or for the Church. Paul no more than got the final words of his testimony out when the crowd roared, "Rid the earth of him! He's not fit to live!"

Today, we could really teach the poor befuddled apostle a lesson. We realize that he really blew it! He must have known that while his testimony had great potential to lead at least some in the crowd to Christ, it had equal potential to offend many in the crowd. It would have been more profitable for him to discuss something like God's great love for the Jewish people. After all, that would have been true; God does love the Jews. Such a smooth presentation would have established very good relations between Paul and the

Jews, and wouldn't they be more likely to listen to someone they liked?

That's the typical modern argument. However, unlike most Christians today, Paul was not concerned with doing things right, the way that guarantees popularity and applause. Paul was concerned about doing right things, the things that please God. He knew God wanted people to meet Him in a powerful way and would not do anything to jeopardize that.

IN THE OLD TESTAMENT

"Now Naaman was commander of the army of the king of Aram. He was a great man in the sight of his master and highly regarded, because through him the Lord had given victory to Aram. He was a valiant soldier, but he had leprosy. Now bands from Aram had gone out and had taken captive a young girl from Israel, and she served Naaman's wife. She said to her mistress, 'If only my master would see the prophet who is in Samaria! He would cure him of his leprosy.' Naaman went to his master and told him what the girl from Israel had said. 'By all means, go,' the king of Aram replied. 'I will send a letter to the king of Israel.' So Naaman left, taking with him ten talents of silver, six thousand shekels of gold and ten sets of clothing. The letter that he took to the king of Israel read: 'With this letter I am sending my servant Naaman to you so that you may cure him of his leprosy.' As soon as the king of Israel read the letter, he tore his robes and said, 'Am I God? Can I kill and bring back to life? Why does this fellow send someone to me to be cured of his leprosy? See how he is trying to pick a quarrel with me!' When Elisha the man of God heard that the king of Israel had torn his robes, he sent him this message: 'Why have you torn your robes? Have the man come to me and he will know that there is a prophet in Israel.' So Naaman went with his horses and chariots and stopped at the door of Elisha's house. Elisha sent a messenger to say to him,

'Go, wash yourself seven times in the Jordan, and your flesh will be restored and you will be cleansed.' But Naaman went away angry and said, 'I thought that he would surely come out to me and stand and call on the name of the Lord his God, wave his hand over the spot and cure me of my leprosy'" (2 Kings 5:1-11).

Today's Christian could set these ancient, well-meaning, but ignorant people from the Bible straight. Observe that the anointed one, the prophet of God, would not come out of his house to greet this man that the Scriptures called "highly-esteemed." We latter-day Christians would know better than to pull such a stunt. Today's "prophet" would not only have come out of the house, he would have network and local news teams there to cover the event so that he could humbly do the work of God.

The great war hero Naaman was expecting to have his pride stroked. He thought there should be great fanfare. He thought the prophet himself should have come out, not just a messenger. Where was the great hoopla that followed a celebrity? To make matters worse, Elisha relayed a very belittling instruction to Naaman: he told him to dip himself in the river seven times. Naaman was expecting something spectacular (perhaps the voice of the archangel and the trumpet of God).

Of course, Elisha was right in what he did. You see, he had something most of us don't have today: he had direct contact with God regularly. He had more to base his actions on than a sermon or a set of general rules taken from the Scriptures. He had the very heartbeat of God on which to base his actions. This is how the prophet knew that God wanted to deal not only with the leprosy of Naaman, but also with his pride. Therefore, Elisha would not come out of his house and thus fuel the fire of Naaman's pride. This is also why he gave him such humbling instructions.

Our media circus, the "right thing to do" in the eyes of men, would have left Naaman to wallow in his pride. In fact, it would have swelled his head even more. When we do things right instead of doing right things, we keep men in their pride and pride keeps men from coming to God. That's the result of doing things **our** way, the "right" way.

TECHNOLOGY IS NOT THE PROBLEM

By now, I'm sure that many of you think this author is against everything and is hungering for a return to the Stone Age, where there's no technology to infect the body of Christ. This is not the case. I'm not against the use of our world's technology in the spreading of the gospel. I believe our ever-increasing technology can become the greatest tool for spreading the gospel Christians have ever had. I'm not against the Church's being a well-polished organization, either. If we're going to even bother doing something that will represent God to our community, we should do it as well as we can. I'm just against one thing: replacing the Holy Spirit.

A PROPER PERSPECTIVE

I read some statistics from a publication called *The Church Around the World*. These figures indicated that South Korea is winning people to Christ at such an alarming rate that the birth rate into Christianity is exceeding that of the natural birth rate. If it continues at its present rate, by the year 2000, every South Korean citizen will be a Christian. The standard response to this startling fact is, "But how...?"

This is the entire point of this chapter. They are growing at such a rate because of prayer. South Korea is doing through prayer what the United States is trying to do through technology. We depend on our technology, not on the Holy Spirit, so we won't pray. Therefore, it is fair to say that technology has become the Holy Spirit of today's Church. However, technology is still not the problem. The problem is that Christians are not praying. With all of her technology, America has the greatest potential for reaching the world with the gospel, but she never will until she combines prayer with her technology. The proper perspective dictates that we have both.

I have seen the two work hand in hand at the church my family and I attend. Every year, the church does two cantatas, one for Christmas and one for Easter. They are without a doubt the most professionally done cantatas in the city. The costumes and sets are worthy of Broadway, and the special effects used have included everything from laser beams to fog produced by dry ice. The cantatas are the single most effective outreaches the church has, bringing more and more people to Christ every year.

However, its success is not due to the sets, nor is it a result of the impressive special effects. Even though the choir begins rehearsals three to four months before the musicals, the golden voices are not the secret either. The drama, though the product of much rehearsing, is not the secret either, as well done as it is. The secret is prayer. The productions are bathed in prayer from the first rehearsal to the last performance. All those involved in them are required to attend the prayer meetings as punctually as the rehearsals. It is those prayer meetings that really secure the blessings that accompany each cantata.

God will not anoint technology. He will not anoint machinery. He will not anoint programs. God anoints men and women who pray. Today—more than programs or state of the art technology—the Church needs saints who will pray, for without them we are doomed to failure. With saints who pray, the power will be restored to our gospel. We will no longer have men and women attending our churches who are bound by life-controlling sin. We will have men and women anointed by God who will know how to pull down strongholds and cast down imaginations.

Particularly, our preachers must be men of prayer. I would much rather be a powerful preacher than a polished pastor, not coming to you with eloquence or wisdom, not coming to you with learned oratory skills, but rather in evidence of the Spirit and power. You must demand that of any man who calls himself a Christian preacher. Not until the Church demands it will we get our pastors praying again.

CHAPTER FIVE

REBUILDING THE ANCIENT BOUNDARIES

> "The great neglect of prayer is a
> grand hindrance to holiness."
> —John Wesley

Have you ever seen anyone pray as much as the victim of some tragedy? The Christian family which has lost its home to a hurricane or tornado, the saint enduring the death of a loved one, the newlyweds who are struck down economically by sudden, unexpected unemployment—they all run desperately to their unchanging, all-knowing Father.

Hard times have a way of drawing us to God. When we experience loss, we realize there is one thing we have which we cannot lose—our relationship with God. In our pain, it is to Him that we turn in prayer. In prayer alone can we wrap ourselves securely in His love and experience His peace to ease our hurts and alleviate our fears. Finally, the stabbing pain of loss caused by the death of that loved one is soothed by the Holy Spirit. All the damage done by the violent storm is repaired as God provides. The Lord graciously and miraculously provides work, and economic security sets in. Life is back to normal again.

Then as good times begin to roll, prayer becomes as much a memory as the disaster that initiated it. As time marches on, hard times set in again from the lack of seeking God. With a renewed attitude of dependence, we return to seeking Him. The Lord hears our prayers and delivers us from our troubles (again). Then when times are good, we stop seeking Him (again). Most of us seem to run through this cycle in our lives. As long as we're enjoying a life of ease, we fail to commune with our God, but the moment we're in a jam, we rush to confer with Him. This cycle repeats itself in our lives with varying frequency. It may occur weekly, monthly, or yearly. When dealing with the Church on the whole, however, the cycle generally repeats itself about once every three generations. The most harmful result of this cycle is that during the largest segments of it, we do not pray.

THE ANCIENT BOUNDARIES

This cycle is nothing new. It marred man's relationship with God throughout the Old Testament, as Nehemiah described in the following prayer: "But they were disobedient and rebelled against you; they put your law behind their backs. They killed your prophets, who had admonished them in order to turn them back to you; they committed awful blasphemies. So you handed them over to their enemies, who oppressed them. But when they were oppressed they cried out to you. From heaven you heard them, and in your great compassion you gave them deliverers, who rescued them from the hand of their enemies. But as soon as they were at rest, they again did what was evil in your sight. Then you abandoned them to the hand of their enemies so that they ruled over them. And when they cried out to you again, you heard from heaven, and in your compassion you delivered them time after time. You warned them to return to your law, but they became arrogant and disobeyed your commands. They sinned against your ordinances, by which a man will live if he obeys them. Stubbornly they turned their backs on you, became stiff-necked and refused to listen. For many years you were patient with them. By your Spirit you admonished them through your prophets. Yet they paid no attention, so you handed them over to the neighboring peoples. But in your great mercy you did not put an end to them or abandon them, for you are a gracious and merciful God'' (Neh. 9:26-31).

As far back as twenty-four hundred years ago, Nehemiah was dealing with the same problem: God's people seek Him in hard times and neglect Him in good times. As a result of the peoples' rejection of the Lord in the good times, hard times set in. In this instance, the ancient Jews' rejection of Him led to the Assyrian captivity of the northern kingdom of Israel and the subsequent take-over of the southern kingdom of Judah by the Babylonians. Jerusalem was destroyed and its remaining inhabitants carried away by their conquerors. However, after the people began seeking God again, their captors allowed some of them to return to their homeland, though still a conquered people.

In the account above, we find that under Nehemiah's leadership, the returned exiles had just finished rebuilding the walls that encompassed Jerusalem. Those walls represented more to those people at that time than walls around our homes would mean to us today. At that time and place, they represented the boundaries in which the residents of the city agreed to live. They weren't imprisoned within these walls, but it was customary for anyone wanting to be identified as a Jerusalemite to live within what those boundaries represented. They represented a certain lifestyle which was to be maintained regardless of where they were.

BOUNDARIES TODAY

Today we don't have physical boundaries we are subject to, but we are to have boundaries—moral and spiritual boundaries. These boundaries identify us as citizens of the kingdom of God, even as the walls of Jerusalem identified citizens of Jerusalem. In past years we Christians were clearly distinguished by (and sometimes scorned for) the boundaries we chose to maintain.

Yet today we have moved our boundaries in spite of clear scriptural admonishment to the contrary. "Do not move an ancient boundary stone set up by your forefathers" (Prov. 22:28).

In our world, Christians indulge in the same ungodly activities as non-Christians to the point that a believer cannot be distinguished from an unbeliever. Popular theology dictates that we Christians can do anything, and God will bless it simply because we are Christians. Life in the church is allegedly nonstop party time. Celebration is the catch word for most Christians. In short, we live in a church without boundaries or limits, and such a church is doomed.

The most common defense for removing the ancient boundaries is that to maintain them would mean a legalistic lifestyle in this, the day of grace. But the fact that we live under grace today does not mean that we should have no limits to our activities. What boundaries were to those living under legalism, conviction becomes to the person under grace. But before we can begin to explore remedies that will restore our boundaries, we must first understand how they were erected.

HOW BOUNDARIES ARE ESTABLISHED

Boundaries are established by convictions. The root of the problem is that today's Church has little or no convictions.

It is because of this that the Church has no boundaries which, in turn, leads every person to do whatever he feels like. The next logical question, "So then how are convictions established?" can be explained in Jesus' own words: "But I tell you the truth: It is for your good that I am going away. Unless I go away, the Counselor will not come to you; but if I go, I well send him to you. When he comes, he will convict the world of guilt in regard to sin and righteousness and judgment: in regard to sin, because men do not believe in me; in regard to righteousness, because I am going to the Father, where you can see me no longer" (John 16:7-10).

Clearly, convictions are established by the Holy Spirit. The Holy Spirit convicts in three areas: in sin, in righteousness, and in judgment. We need to give good thought to the area of righteousness. Today there is very little righteous living. If the Holy Spirit is to convict us of righteousness, why aren't more people convicted of righteousness? Has the Holy Spirit taken a vacation or gone out on strike? No, of course not. But **we** have, judging by our woefully inconsistent prayer lives. Where there is no prayer, there is no Holy Spirit to convict.

Usually, we end up trying to base our actions on the Word of God. We can base our convictions on the Bible, but only if we are a people of prayer. If we aren't a people of prayer, we will not have the guidance and instruction from the Holy Spirit that we need. God never intended for the Bible to be used without His Spirit. Without the Holy Spirit, we can twist the Bible to condone anything we want it to. I have spoken to people who have justified their rock music and even their drinking through the Bible.

The Scriptures have never been a source of conviction apart from the Holy Spirit. The New Testament pharisees are ample proof of this. They knew and could quote all the Old Testament Scriptures, but that knowledge was useless to them because they had a wrong spirit. With their knowledge of the Old Testament, they were able to crucify the Son of God. This is why Jesus said it was to our advantage that He leave to send the Helper. Without the Helper, we could have ended up no better than the pharisees.

Jesus basically said, "I am giving you the Helper so that, among other things, He will convict you of righteousness." Then He said that the reason the Holy Spirit needs to convict us of righteousness is that He (Jesus) was going to the Father and would not be with us anymore. Since He would not be with us anymore, we would need a Helper to remind us of what He was like. The Holy Spirit convicts us of righteousness by reminding us of what Jesus was like.

In addition, Christ is our righteousness. When we have no prayer life, we lose sense of the righteousness of Christ. We begin to do things that Christ would never do, choosing quite on our own what our convictions will be. We couldn't be more wrong. It is not up to us to determine what we will be convicted about. That's up to the Holy Spirit. Our life before we became Christians does not determine what we will or will not be convicted about, either. The Helper is to decide this.

I have heard people say, "Just because I am in the world doesn't mean I am of the world. Just because I am doing things the world does doesn't mean I am of the world." This, too, is a great deception.

Please do not misunderstand our purpose as Christians. Our purpose is not just to figure out what is sinful and what is not. Our primary goal is not to see how much we can get away with, how close we can get to the world and still hang on to our salvation. Our number one purpose is to see how close we can get to God, not how close we can get to the world. The only way to get close to the Lord is in prayer where the Holy Spirit can reveal to us what pleases God and what doesn't. There are no easy shortcuts. That's the only way.

Today it is popular to base our convictions on whether or not there's a chapter and verse that forbids a given activity. We are then left indulging in any activity for which there is not a corresponding biblical "Thou shalt not." This is very far from true conviction which is determined by the Holy Spirit's speaking to us, often telling us to abstain from an activity because it is a weight that hinders us from running the race set before us, not because that activity is an absolute sin. However, if we don't pray, we'll never have that inner sense of what pleases God and what doesn't.

PRAYER DEVELOPS CONVICTION

With an understanding of how convictions are developed, we gain an understanding of how convictions are curtailed. Simply put, if convictions are born out of prayer, they can be killed by prayerlessness.

As we've seen, that's just what happens to most revivals. The founders are pillars of prayer. The first generation of any move of God are people of prayer. They have nothing but God. They have no beautiful buildings or fine musical instruments. They simply have God. Therefore, they must pray. When God begins something, He does it by giving someone some type of revelation or vision. God usually begins with an individual because the masses of people will not respond very quickly. That individual or handful of believers have this great vision before them and, yet, they recognize their own limitations and inabilities. Therefore, they pray that the path God has called them to will be established. Because of their dependency on prayer, they begin to develop convictions which become the boundaries for that movement.

The first generation always establishes the boundaries for their Christian movement. It is very important to realize that the boundaries they set up are based on what would keep them on the path (vision) that God called them to. Their convictions are not based upon sin or the lack of it. Their convictions (boundaries) are determined on the basis of whether or not an activity helps them to stay on the path

God wants them on. Often, it has very little to do with whether or not an activity is specifically denounced as sinful in the Bible. The entire matter is determined by whether that activity would sidetrack them or not.

Their continual prayer and trust in the Lord results in blessings for them and their churches. However, as we discussed earlier, their children are not taught about the importance of prayer. To make matters worse, because of the material blessings granted to their parents and their churches, these children are seldom drawn to prayer. They have fabulous church facilities and can end up relying on them and not God.

CONVICTION BECOMES TRADITION

The Scriptures indicate that God will bless the seed of those who delight in Him (Ps. 112:1,2). The first generation prays and subsequently finds great delight in God. This brings blessings for their children. Remember the cycle? Once we are blessed, we tend to stop praying.

Without prayer, these children do not develop deeply entrenched, Holy Ghost wrought conviction, but they do try to live within the boundaries set by their parents. For the most part, however, they do this to keep tradition ("This is the way Mom and Dad always said it was," or "This is the way it's always been"), not because they are moving at the stirring direction of the Holy Spirit. They might, for example, abstain from going to movie theaters because that's what their parents and everybody in their church had always done. Hence, what was conviction to the first generation (because of prayer) becomes simple tradition to the second (because of prayerlessness).

TRADITION BECOMES A WASTE OF TIME

The third generation surfaces and sees this for what it is: legalism. Following rules and laws without conviction is nothing less than legalism. These new Christians see no purpose in abstaining from something "just because that's the way it's always been." Why should they refuse to go see a movie when all their friends are going to see it? Without prayer, they're in no position to develop any convictions more genuine than those legalistic traditions of their parents.

From lack of prayer (and subsequently conviction), the third generation bases their activities on what is or is not sin. Their mentality is, "If you can't find a Bible verse prohibiting it, then it must be okay to do." They fail to realize that their forefathers based their activities on what would keep them on the path God called them to. They can't believe that their forefathers once had a good reason for avoiding movies. The whole thought of following the ancient ways is lost.

WITHOUT PURPOSE

Without prayer, we lose our reason for being. We live our Christian lives with one rather ignoble purpose: to escape hell. Such a person, who is a Christian with that solitary mission, will base his entire life's conduct on whether something is prohibited as sinful or not in the Scriptures.

This can best be illustrated by comparing it to a wedding night. Imagine that it's my wedding night. My bride and I are having a romantic candlelight dinner. I reach across the table, take both of her hands in mine, and say, "Lou Ann, I love you. I want you to know that no matter how many other women I may be seeing on the side, I'll always love you. In fact, while we're on the subject, just how many affairs can I have with other women before you'll divorce me? I mean, believe me, divorce is the last thing on my mind. It's just that I don't want to stay tied down to one woman, that's all."

Isn't that what we're doing when we base our convictions on what is and is not blatant sin? It's essentially saying, "God, I love You. I really don't want to go to hell.

Lord, while we're on the subject, just how much can I get away with and still make it into heaven?"

What do you think the reactions would be to such statements? My wife's response to my hypothetical statement on our hypothetical wedding night would probably be something like, "I thought you would be interested in doing all you could to make our relationship even more beautiful than it is now!" I think Jesus would have a similar response to that other statement. He would likely say, "I thought you'd be most concerned with seeing how close you could come to Me, not how far away from Me you could get."

THE DILEMMA TODAY

The prophet Jeremiah painted a vivid picture of the dilemma facing the Church today. Notice the prophet's call and the response of the people to it: "This is what the Lord says: 'Stand at the crossroads and look; as for the ancient paths, ask where the good way is, and walk in it, and you will find rest for your souls. But you said, "We will not walk in it." I appointed watchmen over you and said, "Listen to the sound of the trumpet!" But you said, "We will not listen"'" (Jer. 6:16,17).

Today because of prayerlessness, the strong standard of righteous living is hard to find in most of our churches. The ancient boundaries have been forsaken. The result is a chaotic, confused church left to her own resources to establish her convictions, consumed with debating what is and is not sin. The only guide left is the Bible which is a very weak guide without the Holy Spirit as interpreter. Others almost forsake the Bible and insist that all convictions are relative to one's pre-Christian life. Most of these have flocked to nearly every entertainment medium conceivable under the heretical rallying cry, "Satan has had all the good entertainment long enough! It's time for Christians to enjoy it for a while."

A SOLEMN ASSEMBLY

We must get back to prayer, allowing the Holy Spirit to instill immovable conviction and rebuild the ancient boundaries. If we fail to, we are doomed as a church. If we fail to, we have seen our best days spiritually. Without praying moms and dads relentlessly pursuing God, we will raise a generation of children who do not know God. These children will have the same attitude toward sin as the prostitute in Proverbs who wipes her mouth and states, "I have done no wrong."

The Church today is an explosion of celebration. The model Christian life is a showcase of ease and fellowship gatherings. The words "fun, food, and fellowship" are considered to be the high-point of every church bulletin. What the Church really needs today is a solemn assembly, an assembly where our sorrow for our sinfulness can be expressed. Nehemiah and his people held just such an assembly. There was celebration, but the celebration was capped off with introspection.

"On the twenty-fourth day of the same month, the Israelites gathered together, fasting and wearing sackcloth and having dust on their heads. Those of Israelite descent had separated themselves from all foreigners. They stood in their places and confessed their sins and the wickedness of their fathers. They stood where they were and read from the Book of the Law of the Lord their God for a quarter of the day, and spent another quarter in confession and in worshiping the Lord their God" (Neh. 9:1-3).

Our modern-day Church needs a solemn assembly. We don't need another celebration; we need our God. I believe the Lord wants to search our hearts. I also believe He wants a Church without spot or wrinkle.

What are your convictions? Are they based on the direction of the Holy Spirit? Or are they based on your convenience? Or are they based on legalism? Consider these matters in your heart and spend time on your knees consulting the Lord about them. In an effort to make sure that the walls of Jerusalem were not torn down again, Nehemiah found it necessary for the people of God to invest some time in prayer, fasting, and confession. Times haven't changed that much. That's what we need today just as badly.

I'm not saying that we should go back and do things the way they used to be done just because that's the way things were done in "the good ol' days." If we do that, we end up back in legalism. I'm saying that we must get back to prayer. Then we must allow the Holy Spirit to convict us of righteousness. We must allow the Holy Spirit to instill within us conviction that will guide us into a lifestyle that pleases God.

I'm not saying that the third generation is destined to lose out with God. They are simply victims of the cycle we go through. But that cycle can be broken! I feel one of the most important things we can do is to teach our children to pray. We must teach them to pray based on their need for God. We must teach them that they need to pray no matter how their lives are going. Even if they are the most blessed people on earth, they need to pray. Moms and dads, the best way to teach your children to pray is to be parents of prayer. The most effective prayer teachers for them are you! Remember that the biggest reason most children know nothing about prayer today is because Mom and Dad have stopped praying.

God wants to build first-generation believers. Regardless of where you stand chronologically in your Christian heritage, you can become a first-generation believer if you're willing to develop your prayer life. First-generation Christians are simply Christians who pray.

CHAPTER SIX

THE FALL OF THE SLIGHT TOWER

> "How the mighty have fallen!"
> —King David

Throughout the Old Testament, we read references to two types of towers. The first of these is the Strong Tower, one of God's many pseudonyms. The Psalmist speaks of Him when he says, "For you have been my refuge, a strong tower against the foe" (Ps. 61:3). This is just one of many such "Strong Tower" references which are laced throughout the Scriptures.

The second kind is the slight tower, the type that was often erected for the keeper of a vineyard or a flock. Its description as "slight" does not imply that it was either weak or flimsy. As we will see, these towers were nearly impregnable by standards of that day. The prophet Isaiah speaks of it when he says, "He dug it up and cleared it of stones and planted it with the choicest vines. He built a **watchtower** in it..." (Isa. 5:2). Other references to it are made in 2 Chronicles 26:10 and Micah 4:8. Spiritually speaking, a slight tower is a refuge for the pastor (for whom the keeper of a vineyard is symbolic) or for the Church (for whom the flock is symbolic).

In our world towers do not serve the same purposes, nor do they carry they same connotations that they did in the Old Testament. We would be in error if we said that the Sears Tower in Chicago is just an overgrown biblical slight tower. *The International Bible Dictionary* (Logos International, 1977; p.446) helps us bridge this cultural gap with its description of biblical towers. It states, "Towers were erected not only in the outer walls and on the heights within the cities, but along the frontiers of a country, at points where the approach of an enemy could be decried at a distance (see Judg. 9:17; Isa. 21:6-9). A tower afforded refuge to the surrounding inhabitants in case of invasion; and often, when most of a city was subdued, the tower remained impregnable."

Our Strong Tower (the Lord) and the slight tower (the pastor, the Church) both serve a similar function in that they are always to provide a refuge from the enemy. However, only one of these is truly functional today, the Strong Tower, the invincible, eternal Tower. We have refuge in God alone because the slight tower is weak and crumbling, no longer offering the saints a refuge where they may enjoy thoughts that mirror God's thoughts and ways that are the ways of God. No longer can the saint receive the relief he used to in his church because it has adopted the ways of the same world it is supposed to oppose.

In the preceding chapters, we have established the fact that three generations after revival, the believers no longer sense what the first generation did because the latter does not pray. Instead, they cut themselves off from God (that's what not praying does). Consequently, they see no need for holiness in the Church. Yet, it is at this same time that a few sense a need to return to the old ways. They want to know and experience their God, not just promote a moral way of living. What unavoidably ensues is a split.

At the time of this writing, the Church is at a crossroads. There are two diametrically opposed factions developing among born again Christians, one liberal and the other conservative. The liberal faction will promote social causes and morality and do all it can to garner respect from the world. The conservative group will go back to the old ways of prayer and revival.

This pattern can be readily observed in the Bible. Our earlier example of the patriarchs holds true here: Abraham (first generation) and Isaac (second generation) passed on, and then there was a split with Jacob and Esau (third generation). Later, the monarchy of Israel demonstrated this same cycle. After the reigns of David (first generation) and Solomon (second generation), Rehoboam and Jeroboam (third generation) split the nation.

A TOWER DIVIDED AGAINST ITSELF

The most basic cause of all these splits is a lack of unity. In church splits, the third-generation saints lose their unity when they begin to develop vastly different convictions. This potpourri of convictions surfaces because most of the believers base their convictions on elements they do not share in common: their respective pasts and feelings. Everyone has a different past. If everyone bases his convictions on his past, his convictions will, therefore, be as distinct as his past. The same is true of feelings, which are both unique and fickle.

What then of the first generation? Did they not have the same extreme diversity of opinion in the area of convictions? No, they did not. Much like the early New Testament believers, they were of one mind, sharing common beliefs and convictions. These common convictions became the mortar that held their tower together, without which it would have crumbled. They shared common convictions because they received them from a common source: the Holy Spirit, who is, according to John 16:7-11, supposed to give us our convictions.

These convictions were not formed by sitting alone contemplating one's past and one's own thoughts. These first-generation convictions were procured in prayer. Those believers were, by today's standards, "prayer nuts." The standard believer in those days sat alone talking to God, allowing God to forge his convictions. He considered God's thoughts more lofty and more precious than his own, and so based his convictions upon the thoughts of God, not his own.

God is still the Strong Tower, though. He will always be a refuge for His people. However, if the church does not also act as a refuge, people will leave it because they will see little point in going there. Just as one abandons old worn-out useless flashlight batteries, so will the saints of God abandon a church which offers no refuge and whose pastor has no communication with God. This should not be; God and His churches should both serve as an oasis.

THE EYE OF THE PROPHET

A transformation takes place when we spend time with God. Slowly, we begin to think the way God thinks. Our thoughts become His thoughts. For example, the Bible teaches that God hates evil and that the one who truly fears the Lord will hate evil (Prov. 8:13). Yet, today very few Christians hate evil. Most of us can't even grasp the notion of despising and loathing evil as God does. We don't hate evil. We tolerate it. We form indifference toward it. Sometimes, we even flirt with it. Meanwhile, our heavenly Father is light-years away from us in comparison, as a burning rage within Him seethes against evil. The word "hate" is a very strong verb. It transcends "dislike" by miles and is not even in the same category with "indifference." Hate indicates strong, passionate, sometimes uncontrollable emotion. The believer who spends time with God will understand and know this hate. The believer who neglects to spend time with his God will never know or even begin to understand it.

A bond strengthens in prayer between God and the believer. As he begins to think and act more like God, issues around him become very distinct and clear. For him, "to live is Christ." Either issues around him are for God, or they are against God. Nothing is truly neutral for him. Whoever and whatever is not scattering is tearing down. Whatever is not for God is against Him. He sees no middle ground because he evaluates life on God's scale of importance: eternity. On such a scale, many things cease to hold the significance they once appeared to hold.

Isaiah was one such man who had what today would be called "an unbalanced theology." (Yes, the poor man was unbalanced. He was head over heels in love with God. How tragically unbalanced.) In Isaiah 26:8, the prophet said, "Yes, Lord, walking in the way of your laws, we wait for you; your name and renown are the desire of our hearts." In this verse, Isaiah mentioned that he was following God's law, doing things God's way. Furthermore, he said that he wanted God, he wanted His name to be known, and he wanted God to be remembered. These are the things that consumed his life. He didn't waste his life looking forward to payday or the new camel with four on the floor. Those things were part of life, but were fairly unimportant. The spice of life, the reason to be, was God.

Continuing in verse 9, he says, "My soul yearns for you in the night; in the morning my spirit longs for you..." The intensity of this man's desire seems to breathe right through the page as I read it. He wanted God, day and night. There was nothing in the world that he wanted more. His spirit was continually longing after God; his spirit was continually seeking Him.

However, gears seem to shift as verse 9 continues, and many people begin to misunderstand the prophet at this point. "...When your judgments come upon the earth, the people of the world learn righteousness," he says. Here, Isaiah seems rather callous and cold-hearted, almost as if he doesn't care if calamity comes upon the people. It seems that compassion for the sinner was Isaiah's weak spot, but that is usually the case for any believer who has the spirit of a prophet. At the same time we see that Isaiah's words are the result of a heart and a mind that mirror God's in respect to sin.

In verse 10, he concludes, "Though grace is shown to the wicked, they do not learn righteousness; even in a land of uprightness they go on doing evil and regard not the majesty of the Lord." This may seem pessimistic, but it is a sad fact of reality. For many years, our courts in the United States have sentenced our criminals leniently, sometimes giving them little more than a slap on the wrist and a strict warning not to ever, ever let that sort of behavior repeat itself. However, as the Scriptures teach, without judgment, they do not learn, and so crime is running rampant through our nation. That is why Isaiah cries for judgment on God's people because they don't learn without judgment either. It is not a spirit of gloom and doom that motivated him, but a heart for God. He loved God and wanted others to do the same, and he was hurt at how the sinfulness of the world hurt God. He was hurt at how the world did not perceive the majesty of his God.

Because of their lack of prayer, many ministers of the gospel have lost the prophet's eye. Without a longing for God to be glorified and for men to see the majesty of God, there is very little preaching on judgment. When this happens, when ministers stop preaching against sin, their churches become more like the world until they are glutted with the same corruption as the world. Such churches no longer act as refuges. Instead of providing relief from the world, these churches force the world on saints. Clearly the

Church desperately needs men of God—who through spending time with God—see as God sees.

OPEN SEASON ON CHRISTIANS

There is a wild animal preserve just west of Kenosha. It is a refuge, a place of safety for any animal that enters its boundaries. There, the animals can find a haven of rest from mankind. They can relax and find shelter from danger. However, the shelter periodically opens its boundaries to the local hunters. Men and women who are willing to pay the price can have the privilege of hunting the unsuspecting game. Can you imagine the terror that strikes the animals when they suddenly realize that their refuge can no longer provide protection for them?

Animals are not the only ones upon whom "open season" has been declared. Christians come to church because they are weary of this world in which they are strangers. They do not truly understand or like the ways of this foreign land through which they are passing in route to their final destination. They come to church not to forever hide from that world, but to alleviate some of their homesickness for their eternal home and to worship their God. However, it seems that today in too many cases, the spiritual leaders of our tower have declared open season on anyone within the boundaries of its refuge. They have opened the door to Satan and all his cohorts so that they may track down and destroy as many unsuspecting Christians as they can.

Today, our churches are forsaking their standards of holiness and imitating the world in every way possible. These churches have been transformed from refuges from the world into facsimiles of the world. Those who still desire a refuge from the world are left in conflict with the church. For example, I know of parents who oppose Christian rock and roll music on the basis that it is unholy to attempt to recycle the world's ways to worship God. These parents are frequently placed in the unhappy position of opposing their church youth groups. I remember one woman's telling me about her ten-year-old daughter's begging her for a Christian rock and roll tape on the basis that all the kids at church had one. She finally had to give in, even though she suspected the children were being led into a love and desire for a worldly style of music and not into a love and desire for God.

Those who want a refuge from the world's system are not finding it in many of today's churches. They will soon have to either conform or leave the church the same way they would leave any worldly institution that offers them no refuge. If they want a refuge for their children, they will be pulling them out of their youth groups instead of putting them in.

As I was growing up, my parents provided me with a slight tower from many of the things other young people were doing—like dancing. It is unlikely that I'll ever be a dancer. Not only do I have two left feet, but they are both weighted down by forces not yet fully understood by man. At any rate, I was at a disadvantage in junior high school because the sock hop was **the** place to go. Seriously lacking the necessary coordination to successfully attend, I tried to back out of it, but my friends were all pushing me towards it.

I was fortunate for a while. A good way to avoid going to a dance was by not asking a girl to go with me. I could just tell my friends that I didn't have a date. The trouble really began on one dreadful Sadie Hawkin's Day when a girl asked me. What could I do? I was trapped. Well, I was almost trapped. My parents wouldn't allow me to go. They became a refuge for me. I told my would-be date and my friends that my parents wouldn't let me go. I made them sound like the villains. (That was in a by-gone era during which young people basically respected their elders, so it was an excuse they all accepted.) It would have been quite devastating for me had my parents pushed me towards the world.

Today we need pastors and parents who will be slight towers. I took a position as a youth pastor in South St. Paul, Minnesota right after I graduated from Bible college. The pastor there never allowed the boys and girls from the youth group to swim together. Many people thought that was quite outdated and backwards. Yet, he held his position. It was a bit out of date, but I would prefer that situation to one in Florida where I was preaching a seminar. I observed that not only did boys and girls swim together, but the pastor's daughter wore a skimpy bikini that became nearly transparent when it got wet. It is truly unfortunate that we cannot ever seem to reach the happy medium, just in between the extremes. Yet, if we are condemned to extremism, we would be better off extremely conservative than extremely liberal.

WHEN THE CAT'S AWAY...

By the time I accepted Christ at the age of twenty-one, I had already participated in all that the world had to offer me. I had finally been set free. My life was no longer a frustration, seeking and searching for happiness, yet never finding it. I was no longer on the world's treadmill. Then, a year after I was saved, I felt a call to Bible college. In college, I constantly ran into young people who were involving themselves in many of the activities which I had forsaken upon meeting Christ. Whenever I talked to them about these things, they used the old argument about being saved by grace and not by works, adding that I was making a mountain out of a mole hill. I later realized that many of these young people were away from home for the first time in their lives. For the first time ever, they were deciding what their social lives would consist of; their parents weren't. Often these young people were doing things they would never have done had their parents been around. That's just a part of teen life. It's an incarnation of the old cliche, "When the cat's away the mice will play."

Spiritually there is a parallel. I believe that today, many of us are separated from our Parent and are consequently doing many things we wouldn't do if we were in His presence more. Most Christians just flat will not pray. Since they don't pray, they stop caring about glorifying God. That's supposed to be the entire reason for us to live. That passionate desire to glorify God should dictate what we do and what we don't do. Many people argue that they can do a certain thing and yet be saved. This very argument reveals the desire of these people's hearts: to stay saved, not to glorify God. The question should not be, "Can I do this and still be saved?" Rather, we should ask, "Can I do this and still glorify God?"

I'm not talking about legalism. I've discovered that holiness without prayer degenerates into legalism. When we begin to pray, we begin to conduct our life with one goal in mind: to glorify God. The only true life of holiness comes as a consequence of prayer. Subsequently the life of prayer will keep the slight tower strong.

CHAPTER SEVEN
COMING TO GOD IN TRUTH

"Truth received and not responded to means
spiritual declension and loss of capacity."
—T. Austin Sparks

In the fourth chapter of the Gospel of John, we read the account of Jesus and the woman at the well. Jesus had explained to her that if she would drink from what He could give her, she would never thirst again. The woman responded in verse 15 by by saying, "'Sir, give me this water so that I won't get thirsty and have to keep coming here to draw water.' He told her, 'Go, call your husband and come back.' 'I have no husband,' she replied. Jesus said to her, 'You are right when you say you have no husband. The fact is, you have had five husbands, and the man you now have is not your husband. What you have just said is quite true.'"

When Jesus pointed out this woman's sin, she was very quick to admit it. She did not try to whitewash it; she simply said, "I have no husband." She made no attempts whatsoever to cover her actions. She allowed Jesus to reveal the truth about her.

FOOLING GOD

We fool ourselves all the time by trying to fool God. For some reason we are afraid of the truth. We are not truthful with God. We are not truthful with our mates. We are not truthful with our children. The most pathetic situation of all is that we are not truthful with ourselves. Going back to the preceding accounts, we find that Jesus was asked by the woman in verse 20 about the proper way to worship God. Jesus explained in verses 21 and 22, "Believe me, woman, a time is coming when you will worship the Father neither on this mountain nor in Jerusalem. You Samaritans worship what you do not know; we worship what we do know, for salvation is from the Jews."

Many heathens considered certain places particularly holy or fit for the worship of their deities, but Jesus was pointing out that the place of worship was of little importance. The time was at hand in which the spiritual worship of God was about to be established on the earth, and all the rites of the heathen and the Jews were about to be abolished entirely.

Jesus said that worship was no longer going to focus on a place, but rather on an attitude. He clarifies this in verses 23 and 24 in which He states, "Yet a time is coming and has now come when the true worshipers will worship the Father in spirit and truth, for they are the kind of worshipers the Father seeks. God is spirit, and his worshipers must worship in spirit and in truth."

Real worship was going to take place in the heart of man from that moment on. The issue was no longer the outward actions or rituals. The focus would now be who we are in Christ. So when the woman dealt with the place of worship, Jesus did also. However, His focus was entirely different. The woman was dealing with the physical aspects of her relationship with God, but Christ was dealing with the spiritual aspect of that relationship.

True worship of God is being done only by those people who are truthful in their relationship with God. How can we worship a God we are lying to? We will never enter the spirit of worship if we are not truthful with God. The sad fact is that the woman at the well was in better shape than many Christians today. When Jesus pointed out her sin, she acknowledged it.

I once heard Joy Dawson say, "Pride makes truth difficult. Humility accepts it." The proud man will rationalize his sin away. He will have a thousand excuses to explain why he is as he is. But the humble man will simply admit his sin. He can enter into worship because he is not putting up a facade.

A SIN BY ANY OTHER NAME

The world and the Church are working diligently to rename sin. Instead of dealing with the truth of the matter, we rename it. We reason that if a problem can be renamed, then it doesn't have to be dealt with. There are no alcoholics in the Church; there are only "social drinkers." Nobody has a problem with lust; all we deal with is "sexual indiscretion."

One of the main arguments we give to justify our sin is that of using moderation. "Let your moderation be known to all men," is quickly quoted. I find it hard to believe that God would say, "You can sin in moderation." That is not God's direction to His people.

After preaching one evening about the problems of social drinking and casual sex, I was approached by a woman who was determined to convince me that anything done in moderation is acceptable to God. "Is it all right to get drunk in moderation?" I inquired.

"No, that's an absolute," she replied. "The Bible clearly states that we should not get drunk."

"Well, then what about adultery? Can we commit adultery in moderation?" I asked.

"No, that's an absolute too."

I looked at her with no small degree of uncertainty. "Help me understand what you're saying, ma'am. You feel that it's right to do that which leads to an absolute sin, so long as that absolute is not committed?"

She beamed and nodded quickly, saying, "Yes, that's it exactly, so long as you use moderation."

So I said, "Then I can assume that the next time your daughter is out on a date, you don't care if she does everything that leads her to get drunk so long as she doesn't get drunk. And she can do everything that leads to fornication, so long as she doesn't actually fornicate."

Suddenly she didn't like moderation as much as she used to.

Because of the AIDS epidemic, the sexual revolution is said to be over. Yet sexual promiscuity is on the rise in the Church. In addition, for years the Church has been telling the world about the dangers of drugs and alcohol, but now that the world is responding with programs like M.A.D.D. (Mothers Against Driving Drunk) and the "Just Say, 'No'" campaign, we are finding drug and alcohol abuse in the Church, even among our leaders. We are being dubbed liars and hypocrites. We chafe under such accusations. No hypocrite likes his hypocrisy exposed.

The woman at the well was asking Jesus, "What is the proper way to come to God?"

Jesus said. "It's not a matter of actions anymore. It's a matter of the heart." Jesus was trying to make the point that God now lives in the heart, and the heart becomes the place of worship. That's why He said, "You worship what you do not know, but we worship what we know." Every man knows his heart. If his heart is not right with God, if there is no truth, he cannot possibly worship God. Without truth, we will never enter into the true spirit of worship.

When we are living a lie, we find it very difficult to get into the spirit of the place where we are living. When I was ten years old, my mom called me into the house and asked me, "What are you boys doing out in your clubhouse?"

Like most boys my age, I replied, "Nothing."

"I believe you boys are doing something I wouldn't approve of," she persisted. "What is it?"

"If you think we're smoking cigarettes, you're wrong," I answered. My mom didn't even have to bring up smoking cigarettes. I did. I had been living a lie. Once it had been dealt with, I could enter back into the spirit of our home.

SACRIFICE VS. OBEDIENCE

The person who will not deal with truth ultimately deals with sacrifice. In 1 Samuel 15, we find the confrontation between King Saul and the prophet Samuel. God had instructed King Saul to go and utterly destroy the Amalekites. However, when King Saul returned, it was discovered that he had not utterly destroyed them. In verses 10 and 11, we read, "Then the word of the Lord came to Samuel: 'I am grieved that I have made Saul king, because he has turned away from me and has not carried out my instructions.'" The next day, the prophet took this message to Saul. The king greeted Samuel by saying, "'The Lord bless you! I have carried out the Lord's instruction.' But Samuel said, 'What then is this bleating of sheep in my ears?'" (vs. 13,14). Samuel knew that Saul had not fully carried out the Lord's instructions. It is interesting that Saul seemed fully convinced that he had completely fulfilled them. He even said in verse 15, "'The soldiers brought them from the Amalekites; they spared the best of the sheep and cattle to sacrifice to the Lord your God, BUT WE TOTALLY DESTROYED THE REST.'" Samuel then told Saul how God was grieved that He made him king, and Saul still did not get the message. Still fully convinced that half-sin is not full-sin, he said in verse 20,

"'But I did obey the Lord...I went on the mission the Lord assigned me. I completely destroyed the Amalekites and brought back Agag their king.'" There was obviously a lack of understanding between the prophet and the king.

Saul said that he brought back only a few things, and he brought them back only to sacrifice to God. It was then Samuel uttered the famous words in verse 22, "'Does the Lord delight in burnt offerings and sacrifices as much as in obeying the voice of the Lord? To obey is better than sacrifice...'"

Samuel never said God doesn't want sacrifices. It's just that obedience is better than sacrifice because obedience goes before sin; sacrifice goes after it. If Saul had simply obeyed God, it would not have been necessary to make a sacrifice. No matter how we try to justify our sin today, it will be the first thing we sacrifice once God has us on our knees. What we are finding in Christianity today is a people who will search the Scriptures to justify their lifestyles, yet won't search their hearts to find their God.

SINS OF IMMORALITY

Whenever we justify our sin, we will live in a world of sacrifices. Since we don't fully put to death those things which appeal to our flesh, we will constantly be asking God to forgive us for our involvement in them. In Romans 13, we find Paul giving us some godly advice. In verses 13 and 14, he says, "Let us behave decently, as in the daytime, not in orgies and drunkenness, not in sexual immorality and debauchery, not in dissension and jealousy. Rather, clothe yourselves with the Lord Jesus Christ, and do not think about how to gratify the desires of the sinful nature."

Instead of clothing ourselves with Jesus Christ, we make provision for the flesh to fulfill the lust of it. People who have a drinking problem often find they pattern their lives so as to make it easy to drink. I know a pastor who had a remarkable conversation with a man who said he just couldn't kick his drinking habit. "Pastor, I don't know what's wrong with me, but every time I go into a bar, I can't help but take a drink." The lady who can't break her attraction to soap operas frequently has a television set in every room of the house. The man with the lust problem often has a satellite dish in his back yard.

"For the sinful nature desires what is contrary to the Spirit, and the Spirit what is contrary to the sinful nature. They are in conflict with each other, so that you do not do what you want" (Gal. 5:17).

We have this constant struggle going on inside of us. The flesh does not want to seek God, but the spirit does. Which ever one we yield to will determine what becomes of our lives. Two verses after the verse above, Paul tells us what our lives will produce if we give in to the desires of the flesh more than the spirit: sexual immorality, impurity, and debauchery. These are the very things Paul tells us that we will have to turn away from in his letter to the Romans. In a prayerless church, a church that gives itself more to the desires of the flesh than the spirit, sexual immorality is quite common.

King Saul was told to utterly destroy the Amalekites. They were a very immoral people. They represent the constant struggle man has with his flesh. Even as they were constantly fighting with God's people, so does our flesh. Saul's refusal to totally destroy the Amalekites can be likened to our struggle against our flesh. Today we keep hard-core pornography out of our Christian homes, but we watch **"Dallas"** on our televisions. We still make provisions for the flesh and, subsequently, we constantly struggle with the grip the flesh has on us. Until we obey, we will live in a world of sacrifices.

THE SACRIFICE GOD ACCEPTS

King David lived in a world of sacrifices. David had his problems with obeying God. However, David had a heart for God and eventually learned what God was looking for. In Psalm 51:17 we read, "The sacrifices of God are a broken spirit [the true worshipers of God come to Him in spirit]; a broken and contrite heart [they come to God in truth], O God, you will not despise."

David was honest with God. We will never shock God with truth. If we decide to tell God about our problem with sin, we will not set God back on His throne in astonishment. Remember, God is not about to say, "I never knew that about you." He knows all about us and is waiting for us to come to Him with our shortcomings so that He can help us overcome them. But if we don't bring the truth about our sin to God, we will forfeit His help to overcome it.

Each of us must ask, "Do I want to be one of the true worshipers of God?" If we do, then we must go to Him with our hearts open. We must allow God to minister to us. God never reveals sin to bring judgment upon us. God reveals sin for one purpose: to bring us to repentance and reconciliation.

CHAPTER EIGHT

YOUR CONCEPT OF GOD

"There was no fire, no light in the room; nevertheless, it appeared to me as if it were perfectly light...It seemed as if I met the Lord Jesus Christ face to face."
—Charles Finney, in prayer

What is your concept of God? What do you believe about God? You may wish to carefully consider these questions before you read this chapter because they form the heart of it. Your concept of God will determine your faith in God and your worship of Him. That makes your concept of God very important and an understanding of where it comes from even more important.

WHERE CONCEPT COMES FROM

In his book *Whatever Happened to Worship*, A.W. Tozer

develops an interesting thought by saying, "No church can rise above its religion." Most people receive their concept of God from their denomination. A person is generally able to have faith in God only to the degree that his denomination does. Generally, a person who attends a Roman Catholic or Lutheran church will not believe in divine healing or speaking in tongues. Why? Simply because that person's denomination does not teach it. On the other hand, a person who attends a Pentecostal church will believe most fervently in such things. Why? Again, because his denomination teaches it. Our faith in God is limited to our concept of God, and that concept of God generally comes from our denomination.

However, twentieth-century technology has brought us another source from which we may gain our concept of God: the electric church (Christian TV and radio). It has allowed Christians to see beyond their denomination. It is causing church growth and church splits, but in either case, it is forming Christians' concept of God.

Also, influential for those of us who have been born again is that person who led us to the Lord. We usually believe as that person does. This was true for me. Everything I believed hinged on what Bill Ellerman, my spiritual father, believed. If Bill didn't believe something was so, it just plain wasn't so. I became very dependent upon Bill, unable to stand alone. I could see only as much of God as he saw.

ELIJAH AND ELISHA

"As they were walking along and talking together, suddenly a chariot of fire and horses of fire appeared and separated the two of them, and Elijah went up to heaven in a whirlwind. Elisha saw this and cried out, 'My father! My father! The chariots and horsemen of Israel!' And Elisha saw him no more. Then he took hold of his own clothes and tore them apart. He picked up the cloak that had fallen from Elijah and went back and stood on the bank of the Jordan.

Then he took the cloak that had fallen from him and struck the water with it. 'Where now is the Lord, the God of Elijah?' he asked. When he struck the water, it divided to the right and to the left, and he crossed over" (2 Kings 2:11-15).

Elisha had just witnessed the power of God. God had displayed His strength in parting the waters, in taking Elijah up in the chariot of fire, and yet Elisha called out for the God of Elijah. Why didn't he cry, "Where is the Lord, my God?" It is because Elisha was so dependent on Elijah for his concept of God, even as I was dependent on Bill. Hence, we see that even as far back as 800 B.C. (the time of Elisha), God's people have relied on one another for our concept of God.

This is not bad in and of itself. We all begin this way, but God expects us to reach a point at which we develop our own concept of Him. Unfortunately, this is where most Christians are today. They see only as much of God as their spiritual parent, their pastor, or their favorite television evangelist.

HEARSAY VS. REVELATION

What I just described is a hearsay concept of God. It is a concept of God that is built upon what a third party (i.e., not you or God, the first and second parties) has to say about God. I'm not saying that such concepts of God contradict God's true nature or character. They may or may not. However, that's not the real problem. The real problem with a hearsay concept of God is that it's like seeing a Xerox copy of a DaVinci painting instead of the original masterpiece. Although the Xerox copy probably won't distort the painting beyond recognition, it just won't do it justice. There will be things in the original that won't be seen on that black and white copy. The copy, at best, will give the casual observer a basic idea about what the painting is.

As I said, my concept of God was by and large a theological assent to what my spiritual parent believed. But then, God placed in me a craving to know Him for myself. I knew a lot about God from what I heard my spiritual elders say, but I didn't **know** Him. Similarly, you might say, I know a lot **about** the president of our country from what I've heard about him on the news, but I don't **know** the president. I was tired of knowing **about** God. I wanted a direct revelation of God from **God**—not from another Christian. I was consumed with this craving to know Him for myself, and there were two things that set me on my way to begin to know God through revelation, not hearsay: prayer and the Bible.

PRAYER

I don't believe it is possible to build a relationship with anyone (especially God) if we don't converse with that individual. When we want to build a relationship with a person, we talk, we do things together, and usually find that as we spend more time with that person, we become more like him or her.

This wonderful communication we treat so mundanely is our opportunity to interact with God. It's also His opportunity to interact with us.

In writing a book so heavily built upon prayer, I realize that I have the potential to down play the importance of God's Word. There's nothing I want less to do because without the Bible we develop an unbalanced life just as we do if we read the Bible without praying. Only with proper balance of both the Word and prayer can we develop a correct concept of God.

INACCURATE CONCEPTS OF GOD

For the past two decades the focus of the Church has been on the Word of God to the exclusion of prayer. This has resulted in a very human concept of God. The Word of God deals with the fleshly aspect of God. The Word became flesh. Because of a focus on God's Word only, we have developed a very fleshly approach to God. That is why there are ministries today which teach strictly about what God can do to satisfy our flesh.

It is astonishing how much theology has been formulated to deal exclusively with the flesh, or material comfort. We have become far more concerned with comfort than character. The Word of God gives us the human concept of God. Prayer reminds us of the deity of God. Today because of the lack of prayer, we have lost sight of the deity of Christ. From the lack of prayer and the Word, we have developed a concept of God that is off-centered and has given birth to dubious ministries like Christian rock music. Ministries with a wrong concept of God transfer that wrong concept to those they bring to Christ. Mistakes like these are very serious because our concept of God determines how we worship God.

If we are not seeing God as He is and developing a concept of Him that is true to His nature, then we will see Him as He is not. The result will be that we will offer Him offensive worship ("strange fire") that clashes with His true nature, and that is just what has happened, just as it did three thousand years ago when the children of Israel were wandering through the desert.

"Aaron's sons Nadab and Abihu took their censers, put fire in them and added incense; and they offered unauthorized fire before the Lord, contrary to his command. So fire came out from the presence of the Lord and consumed them, and they died before the Lord. Moses then said to Aaron, 'This is what the Lord spoke of when he said: "Among those who approach me I will show myself holy; in the sight of all the people I will be honored"'" (Lev. 10:1-3).

Notice Moses' response to Aaron when he said, "This is what the Lord spoke when he said, 'Among those who approach me, I will show myself holy.'" In essence Moses was telling Aaron not to be surprised about what happened to his boys. God had said that anybody who worships Him must treat Him as holy. Aaron's sons came before God offering Him strange fire or worship that is not in character with who God really is. God will not accept worship that is contrary to His true nature.

Entire ministries (such as Christian rock music ministries) are rising and propagating concepts of God that have been dictated by people's feelings about God. These ministries are not spreading a concept of God that they have received from God, but rather are distributing a concept of God which reinforces their own interests and lifestyles. People who are brought to the Lord by these ministries end up with the same concept of God as the one espoused by these ministries. It is not just a matter of whether they are bringing people to Christ. It is a matter of what kind of concept of God they are developing in young minds. Today we have a rock-and-roll God.

Converts won through rock music will defend it for two basic reasons:

1. People generally regard anything that brought them to the Lord as being sacred;
2. Christianity as they know it must, somehow, by definition include Christian rock music. As long as they've been Christians, rock music has been part of the normal scene. In a way, it is part of their heritage, so they will defend it just the same as any person will defend his religion.

Many parents have asked me what they can do about their children's zeal for Christian rock music. They are indeed faced with a dilemma. They don't want their children listening to secular rock music, so they see Christian rock music as the lesser of the two evils. At the same time, they know in their hearts that neither "evil" is suitable for true believers.

I would rather have my son listen to secular music than to music by "Christians" who do not present a true picture of Jesus Christ. He will know that the secular music is the product of an unregenerate heart and won't equate it with

God. However, he will identify the "Christian" music with God, a very serious error. It is my desire that he listen to neither, but the secular music, I believe, is the lesser of two evils.

The Bible states that God hates the corrupt system of the unsaved world and that anyone who is a friend of that world is an enemy of God (1 John 2:15). How could anyone read that and then recycle the very thing God hates in order to draw people to Him? That is strange fire. It is strange worship.

Historically, the worship of the Church has not been a puppet of the secular world's latest trends. It was a manifestation of a revelation of God, generally in the midst of a tremendous revival.

Consider the experience of Isaiah recorded in Isaiah, chapter 6. He had a supernatural revelation of God in which the Lord was surrounded by seraphim crying, "Holy, Holy, Holy is the Lord of hosts!" That was what he wrote down—that was revealed to him.

A great number of our classic hymns are the work of Charles Wesley. He did not write them to make a quick buck, nor did he write them to find favor with the world. Instead, he wrote them as the Church was revived by a new revelation of God. God revealed Himself to what was becoming an increasingly stale Church in a new way. (We usually refer to this as "revival.") This new exciting revelation of God motivated Charles Wesley to write songs. As his brother Jonathan was bringing the revival in with his preaching, Charles was writing songs of worship that boldly declared praises to the special attributes of God which He revealed. Those hymns were a result of a concept of God that was based on revelation knowledge.

We can see this same thing in the worship of Martin Luther. He wrote "A Mighty Fortress Is Our God" as a result of a revelation of God. On the night before he was to appear before an inquisition of the Roman Catholic Church, he spent much time fearfully praying to God, and, in response,

God revealed Himself as a "mighty fortress," in the words of the Psalmist. Most of our worship today is, sadly enough, a result of "feelings" about God with no real heaven-sent revelation.

HOW DO YOU SEE GOD?

How do you see God? Is your spiritual sight limited to what another person sees? Are you spending time with God in prayer? Are you studying the Bible? Is your concept of God based on that prayer and Bible study?

It is crucial that you determine answers to these questions because the way you see God will determine your degree of faith as well as your worship.

Do you see God as **Elohim**, the Creator, the One who has absolute, unqualified, unlimited power? Do you see Him as the One who is willing to put forth power on your behalf?

Do you see God as **El**, the strong One? In Psalm 22:1, the Calvary Psalm, Christ in His agony cries out to this God.

Do you see God as your **Jehova-Jireh**, the Provider? I remember when my wife, Lou Ann, and I first went out on the road with our ministry full-time. We had no guarantee of any income. Some of those first seminars took place in churches so small we could count the congregations on one hand. I remember driving from Wisconsin to Utah to do a seminar for four people. My great need drove me to prayer where I gained a new revelation of God as my Provider, and God always came through.

Do you see God as your Healer, **Jehovah-Rophi**? I don't mean to ask if you see Him as **a** Healer. I mean to ask if you see Him as **your** Healer?

God wants us to have our own revelation of Him, not some warmed-over revelation that was somebody else's. But make no mistake about it: the only way we'll ever have our revelation of God is through prayer and Bible study. There's no short cut. If we are not pray-ers, we have no business trying to minister to others. If we don't see God as He is, how can we show others how God really is?

We may be leading them into false worship. Our worship is an expression of our concept of God. Do you believe God likes to "get down and boogie?" Or do you believe He is high and lifted up, with His train filling the temple as angels are calling out, "Holy, Holy, Holy is our God!"

WHAT SHOULD WE DO?

What should we do to get a revelation of God? We should do the same thing the men of God in the Bible did to get their revelations of God. When Moses met God, he spent forty years in the desert getting to know Him. Then and only then, did he become the greatest leader the ancient Israelis every had. He was able to lead others because God was leading him. What about Paul? When he met Jesus, he went out into the desert where he spent three years getting to know God. After that—not before—he emerged as the most prolific writer of the New Testament. He could show others God because he let God show Himself to him.

CHAPTER NINE

GOD WORKING IN US

> "For it is God which worketh in us both to
> will and to do of his good pleasure."
> —Paul, the apostle

As a young preacher right out of Bible college, I had the same types of thoughts toward my own ministry as other young preachers did about theirs. We all wanted to change the world. We all wanted to take Billy Graham's place. From the moment I entered the ministry, I prayed that God would make my ministry an effective one. As I discovered the importance of prayer, I continued praying that God would make me an effective minister, but when I did so, I began sensing God saying over and over, "Seek Jesus; seek My Son." I started to learn that God wanted to work in me while all I had been wanting God to do was work through me. Wanting God to just work through us is a selfish desire for personal success and comfort. Wanting God to work in us, however, is a long hard pursuit of character development.

I remember being an associate pastor in Minnesota, watching evangelists come through my church and wishing I could be as effective as they were because we had some of our best services when they preached. But deep down inside of me, I wanted to be more like them more because I wanted everybody to think that I was a very spiritual preacher. That motivated me more than really wanting to serve God through my ministry. I didn't realize it then, but true spirituality cannot be measured by the degree to which one is successful in ministry.

EMPIRES THROUGH GIFTEDNESS

One's natural abilities can build religious empires. Many talented ministers have built huge ministries on their own giftedness. But Paul said, "...If I have a faith that can move mountains, but have not love [if we have not developed the character of Christ], I am nothing" (1 Cor. 13:2). Nothing will last that is not built upon Christ-like character. Many large ministries have crumbled for lack of Christ-like qualities such as self-control.

In 1987, the scandal involving Jim Bakker snowballed into a "holy war" when Jerry Falwell took over PTL and was later accused of trying to steal the ministry from the Bakkers. Many accusations were made between the two factions and threats of legal action were made. If everyone had been concerned about developing God's character in their lives, there would have been no need for vengeance, nor any need to fear a party's trying to "steal everything." When our ministry is built on the character of God, it will go on without us. The Rev. Owen Carr labored for many years at his church in Chicago with little success. Then when revival came to that church, he sensed God's calling him to a different work, so he began arguing with God: "If I leave now, the revival will die," he said.

God replied, "If this revival is dependent on you, then it needs to die."

Owen went on to start a television ministry in Chicago. Both the church and the TV ministry are still doing great things today even though Owen is no longer involved with either.

It is very common to hear people say that a certain ministry couldn't exist without the person who founded it. That may be true if mere man is the force behind it. However, no ministry will die if it has been built upon the character of Christ. But without that character, the ministry can die and the leader can lose his livelihood.

THE KEY TO EFFECTIVENESS

The key to an effective ministry is not God's working through us, but His working in us. When a person spends great amounts of time in prayer, God works in him, changing him, conforming him to the likeness of Christ. Because God is working in him, that man's ministry is effective. People see Jesus in that man and respond to the conviction of the Holy Spirit in that man's life. That is what the world needs from us today. They've already been exposed to ministries which only tout man's giftedness, and these ministries have ended up at war with each other and caving in on themselves. As a result of this exposure, the world is reluctant to believe anything Christians have to say.

WHAT GOD SEES OR WHAT MAN SEES?

When we focus on God's working through us, we primarily center in on what man sees, but when we focus on God's working in us, we concern ourselves primarily with what God sees. If all we do is concern ourselves with what man sees, then all we need to do is be careful and not get caught. In my book *Prayer Can Change Your Marriage*, I admitted that I was sneaking off to see "R" rated movies and having problems with the flesh. I used to do those things because I was sure I wouldn't be caught. Obviously, I was concerning myself only with what people saw.

But then I began to seek God. I began to pray, and suddenly, I found myself under the conviction of the Holy Spirit to such an extent that I decided to confess my weakness to my wife. I even published it in a book. God has used that confession to minister to countless men and women because when God prompts us to repentance, all men accept it. But when we're caught in our sin and forced to admit it after the fact, few people accept it. They're always wondering, "Would they have confessed their sin if it hadn't been exposed? Did they really repent?"

A PERSON OF PRAYER

If God wants to work through me, I must be a man of prayer. Proverbs 16:6 teaches us that "...through the fear of the Lord a man avoids evil." Prayer is the active practice of fearing God. To fear God is to pray. It develops great reverence for God. Suddenly, we conduct ourselves according to what God sees, not what man sees. When we live in the fear of the Lord, we turn from iniquity. When we live in the fear of man, we have to get caught before we quit. The love of man, even love of our own family, will never keep us from sin. We must develop a love for God.

"Different kinds of fruit trees can quickly be identified by examining their fruit. A variety that produces delicious fruit never produces an inedible kind. And a tree producing an inedible kind can't produce what is good. So the trees having the inedible fruit are chopped down and thrown on the fire. Yes, the way to identify a tree or a person is by the kind of fruit produced" (Matt. 7:17-20; LB).

The kind of fruit we produce is determined by how much time we spend with God. He must always be our objective, not just an effective ministry. We must let our ministry flow out of a right relationship with God.

CHAPTER TEN

DOING THE RIGHT THING THE WRONG WAY

> "When we argue, it is about the means, not the end."
> —Aristotle

"This piece of legislation is absolutely crucial," said the host of a Christian television program I happened to tune into. "Congress will be voting on this bill within the week, and we need Christians all over this country praying around the clock." As he was delivering this plea for prayer, a viewer telephoned to ask what else could be done. "At this point, all we can do is pray," replied the host. "I know we can do that," she interrupted, "but I'm a person of action. I need to do something." I grimaced, releasing a small sigh, and clicked off the television as I realized the unfortunate significance of that little dialogue.

That woman's comment very adequately sums up the modern Church's attitude toward prayer. It has been my experience that a great number of people today have the notion that prayer is the same as doing nothing. That woman went out of her way to make a distinction between praying and actually accomplishing something. It is believed that the two are worlds apart and as different as night and day. She said she knew she could pray, but pointed out that she'd rather **do something.**

The premise here is that prayer is a nice, spiritual thing to do, something we certainly **should** do if we're Christians; no question about it. However, if there's really something important hanging in the balance, we're going to have to be "realistic." We're going to have to "live in the real world." When there's a task to be accomplished, "we don't need idealistic dreamers who build kingdoms upon clouds. It's nothing against those idealists (they really do mean well!), but what we really need in that hour of importance are realists, not dreamers. We need an army of radical militants who will march out into the world, swords drawn, and see that goal achieved if it takes every ounce of their strength to do it!"

What about prayer? Where does that come in?

"Prayer? Oh, yes, well, that. You ought to pray. A little added insurance sure can't hurt, and when all else fails, it gives you a 'Plan B' to fall back on."

The prevalence of this erroneous theory is a tragedy of the third degree. Prayer is the most formidable weapon with which the Church has been endowed, yet it is the least relied upon. Our ability to pray is our own private line to God, He who relies upon no one, He who is completely self-sufficient, He whose resources are endless, whose powers are limitless. Yet, today prayer is observed as a religious rabbit's foot. It's a little extra added insurance or a last resort.

Why do people have this attitude? It's mostly because they don't pray. If we don't pray, we don't see the Lord's mighty response to prayer. Since they see no response, no accomplishments they can attribute to prayer, they assume that it's because prayer just doesn't work and doesn't really accomplish anything. The average person says, "I've never seen an astonishing answer to prayer." The reason this average person has never seen an astonishing answer to prayer is that there are little or no prayers for the Lord to answer.

SALVATION OR REHABILITATION?

Life in a democratic society has produced some regrettable side-effects on the Christian Church. A group of sign-toting, slogan-quoting political lobbyists has emerged as a dominant force in the Church. They're quite prone to circulating petitions and picketing institutions that violate Christian moral codes. In short, these people are out to rehabilitate the world. They are endeavoring, primarily through political means, to force the world to abandon all of its evil practices and adopt Christian ways. This seems to me to contradict the philosophy of life Jesus espoused.

"For the Son of Man came to seek and to save what was lost" (Luke 19:10).

Jesus had no intentions of trying to rehabilitate the population of the planet to create some kind of utopia where His moral convictions would be followed to the letter. Jesus came to **save** the world, not to rehabilitate it. He came to reconcile men with God and, in the process, bring the world everlasting life. Reconciling men with God, bringing men into an eternal fellowship with their Creator, was the heartbeat of our Saviour. That's what He spent His life doing and ultimately gave His life to accomplish.

In the area of morals, He expressed concern only for those who called themselves His disciples or referred to themselves as God's people. Paul followed a similar rule of thumb: "What business is it of mine to judge those outside the church? Are you not to judge those inside? God will judge those outside" (1 Cor. 5:12-13).

In the New Testament Church, Paul was concerned only with the morals of those in the Church. He wasn't out crusading against all the atrocities that were commonplace in the Roman Empire, and the Empire was much more decadent than the United States is today. Paul's only concern for the world was that those in the world be reconciled with God. After that they would be expected to lead godly lives—not before.

SO? IT'S NOT HURTING ANYBODY!

So often I hear people say, "So? It's not hurting anybody! Maybe Paul and Jesus didn't do this, but that doesn't make it wrong. If it was hurting my witness, it would be wrong, but this isn't."

But it is hurting your witness and possibly the witness of other Christians who are having nothing to do with it. As Christians, we should be identified as ones rich in the fruit of the Spirit: love, joy, peace, and so on. When people see us, **that's** what they should associate us with. They might say, "Boy, so-and-so is sure a religious fanatic," but in the same breath they'll have to admit, "but he sure is a loving person—he'd give you the shirt off his back. And he actually seems to have a real peace about him." Unfortunately, many Christians today are not viewed with such esteem. Why? Because they don't exude love or any other fruit of the Spirit. They, instead, present themselves as political bullies who don't appear to care about anybody but themselves and their moralizing.

The following excerpt from a newspaper article entitled "The Angry Fundamentalist's Quest to 'Capture a City for Christ'" illustrates this perfectly:

"...While different fundamentalist groups display varying degrees of militancy, that single characteristic—anger—sets fundamentalists apart...To the fundamentalist, the world seems to be floundering in chaos. He or she is angry at the world and believes God is, too...Fundamentalists offer the world a nostalgic vision of order—of moral absolutes, of religious certainty, of rigid conformity to certain favorite standards. To submit to this magnificently ordered world is called 'being born again.'...What would it mean to 'capture a city for Christ?' It would mean to impose on that city the values and the beliefs of the fundamentalist...The gospel is not so much a word of comfort as a weapon used to do battle against the world that the fundamentalist fears..." (**Minneapolis Star Tribune**; Aug. 17, 1987).

Many immediately cry, "Oh, what do you expect to hear from that devil-inspired media!" That's not a very intelligent attitude. I have known some non-Christian journalists, and I feel that I am qualified to state that not all journalists are plotting the demise of fundamentalist Christianity. Did you ever stop to consider that just maybe they're calling the shots the way they see them? In the article above, I believe the reporter is describing the Church as he sees it. Why do media representatives see it that way? Because that's how we show it to them.

Sadly, many people today outside the Church think that we in the Church are trying to violate the **right** to self-determination that God gave them. They are convinced that we are trying to coerce them into something they don't want.

This doesn't mean that we should never be involved in the promotion of morality on given issues. It just means that such involvement should be aimed at the goal Jesus gave His life for: the reconciliation of man with His God. We should never be trying to rehabilitate the world. We should be expending our energy to see the world come to know Christ as the Saviour. It does no good for us to rid the world of all its sinful activities if the world has not been reconciled to the Lord and accepted Jesus' atoning work for its salvation.

Everything we do involving our relationship with the world should be aimed at salvation. Our Christian labors shouldn't be designed just to create an unsaved world that doesn't offend our delicate sensibilities.

THE GREAT COMMISSION OR THE GREAT COERCION?

While I was teaching a prayer seminar in a church in the Midwest, I became aware of a struggle the church was involved in with its community. The community wanted to open a new bar in town and, of course, the church was opposed to the idea. Therefore, the church circulated a petition aimed at preventing the establishment of a new tavern. However, since the community was small and the church was large, enough people just within the church signed the petition to prevent the liquor license from being granted.

The congregation was overjoyed, thoroughly convinced that they had won a resounding victory. Their neighbors, on the other hand, were not pleased. In fact, many were seething with hatred toward the church. Was this a victory? No! Instead of turning the community to Christ, they hardened the community's hearts toward the church. All that church showed the townspeople was her ability to form a strong political block. But the residents of that area were angry that the church was strong-arming them, foisting their morals on people who did not want them. Just what does that accomplish for God? How is eternity different? Nothing even changed in that community during the here and now. Many people continued to drink at the bar a mile down the road.

I can't say that opposing the establishment of a new tavern is in itself wrong, but that community's reason for opposing it was wrong. They just wanted their will imposed on the community regardless of that community's wishes. The only right motivation for this opposition would have been to, in the end, show people Christ. All that church wanted to do was to showcase her piety and her political power as a special interest group, and that isn't even close to showing people Christ.

When we attempt to bring people to Christ, we engage in a spiritual battle. When we attempt to flex our political muscle, we're just in a physical battle: get enough people to sign a petition, and the battle is won. A spiritual battle can't be fought that way. The true victories cannot be won by means of legislation or political influence.

WAGING WAR WITH A WATER PISTOL

As Christians, we are waging a war which Paul maintained is "...not against flesh and blood, but against the rulers, against the authorities, against the powers of this dark world and against the spiritual forces of evil in the heavenly realms" (Eph. 6:12). So, when we engage in a flesh-and-blood battle, we affect only the physical world. The church I mentioned only affected the physical world by preventing a bar from opening. Unfortunately, because they were fighting a physical battle, there was no way for them to touch man's spirit, and that should be our goal.

We know we can't achieve our goal of changing a man's spirit through fighting this physical war. So, just how can we reach the spirit of man? The only way to change man's spirit is through showing him the power of God. "I became a servant of this gospel by the gift of God's grace given me through the working of his power. Although I am less than the least of all God's people, this grace was given me: to preach to the Gentiles the unsearchable riches of Christ, and to make plain to everyone the administration of this mystery, which for ages past was kept hidden in God, who created all things. His intent was that now, through the church, the manifold wisdom of God should be made known to the rulers and authorities in the heavenly realms" (Eph. 3:7-10).

In this letter to the church at Ephesus, Paul clearly states that the Church is supposed to make known God's strength and wisdom, not the Church's strength and wisdom (which are manifested through purely political exhibitions). And who are we supposed to make it known to? To the "rulers and authorities in the heavenly realms." And just who are they? By also considering Ephesians 6:12, you will see that these rulers are spiritual forces that unsaved man is being controlled by.

Paul was most concerned about the spiritual world because it controls the physical world. He realized that all the evil things he saw were a result of the spiritual things he couldn't see. If he were here today, I believe he would say something like, "You foolish Christians! Who has bewitched you? You may go on attacking simplistically! Yes, continue your democratic picketing and your twentieth-century lobbying! But mark my words, you shall accomplish nothing because the problems of mankind are spiritual and can only be resolved spiritually. How can problems that are caused spiritually be resolved physically? Go on and fight this way and you will be waging a full-scale attack on the enemy's camp armed with only a water pistol."

It is essential that we realize that our greatest strengths do not reside in what we can see with our eyes. Gideon learned this the hard way. God instructed him to attack the Medianites, so Gideon gathered all his men together for the battle. However, God interrupted Gideon's preparations for battle to point out that Gideon had a problem. He told Gideon—get this—that he had **too many** men for the battle and that he would have to get rid of some of them!

Can you imagine our reaction today? Doubled over in convulsive laughter we would cry, "Oh, that's rich, Lord! Who says You don't have a sense of humor?" We would naturally assume "the more, the better." But God wanted not only the Medianites to see His power, but also Gideon and his men. God ordered Gideon to decrease the size of his army "...In order that Israel may not boast against me that her own strength has saved her" (Judg. 7:2).

Why is it that we trust our own strength over God's?

It is simply because we generally don't pray regularly, and as a result, we forfeit an understanding of God's power.

THE RIGHT THING THE RIGHT WAY

Suppose that church members in the Midwest had expressed their concern to the community and explained why they were concerned. In a loving way, they could have mentioned the societal ills that spring from taverns, such as drunk driving, stabbings, shootings, etc. Then, if the community did not support their action, they could have said—without malice or arrogance— "Very well, but we're going to pray and ask God to keep this bar from opening." Then suppose that through some odd turn of events, the bar did not open (I call this "answered prayer").

If the church had selected this course of action, much more would have been accomplished; the people would have seen the power of God. They couldn't credit the church people with the bar's failure to open because they didn't do anything but pray, so they'd have to recognize God as the agent. As it was, nobody saw what the church did as having anything to do with God.

Any group can picket, protest, and pass petitions. The thing that sets us apart is that only we can show the world the manifold wisdom of God.

I'm sure that some of you are saying, "That's all very idealistic. It would be great if that's how things would go, but what if God would not have done anything, and the bar would have opened?"

Allow me to add some questions like: "What if the Red Sea had not parted before Moses and the children of Israel?" and even "What if Jesus had not risen from the dead?" The scenario that I have proposed for that church above is based on the prayers of the people of God. The reason many people say that what I have proposed is idealistic is that they don't understand God's power in response to prayer. They have never experienced prayer as the Church's most powerful weapon, and so they can't imagine its being so.

I have been to churches all over this country, and I have observed that prayer meetings are the least attended gatherings of them all. It seems that pastors today just cannot call their people to prayer and receive a response from them. This leaves us with only one option: fight a spiritual battle with physical weapons. Bear in mind that pornography really isn't the problem. Bars really aren't the problem. The heart of man is the problem. It is separated from the Creator and subsequently, has developed a great capacity for evil.

As I have delivered this message in various churches, I have certainly met with opposition. I have been told that picketing and so on does indeed achieve desirable results. I have been informed that it "makes people more aware." So, just what exactly is it that this awareness accomplishes for God? Suppose that we made the entire world aware of the horror of sin to the point where all the nations of the world sided with us and agreed with us completely. Suppose that every person adopted the Golden Rule as a personal code of ethics. What would be the good of this if it didn't turn anyone to God? So what if a person is moral? So, he may get the executive suite in hell. What's the point of that?

Paul said that we are not to be struggling with flesh and blood, and yet a variety of church groups are trying to get a half-nelson on the flesh-and-blood proprietor of the local pro shop. Paul was struggling with heavenly powers, not their physical manifestations. Paul was playing for keeps, for eternity.

A QUESTION OF RIGHTS

I recall speaking to a woman who, before she became a Christian, had owned two topless bars in Texas. One evening as she was on her way to open her bars, a man stopped her and began to tell her about Jesus: why He lived and why He died. The Holy Spirit went to work, and that evening she accepted Christ on the spot, right there on the sidewalk. From that moment, she knew that she could never open those bars again. Since then, those buildings have never been used for that purpose. That is the result of a changed heart.

Let's suppose, just for a moment, that she didn't meet that Christian who explained the gospel to her that night. Instead, let's suppose that she ran head on with a group of militant Christians picketing her bars. What do you think would have happened? Do you think she would have run toward them crying, "Life! Life! Eternal life!" like John Bunyan's character in *Pilgrim's Progress*? Neither do I, although I'm sure she would have run toward them yelling (probably something censorable).

She would have been outraged, insisting that she had the right to do whatever she might wish to do on her property. She would have wondered where that group of religious fanatics got off trying to force her to give up her rights. At best, that's what such a group of picketers would be demanding that she do: yield her rights. Unfortunately, people don't like giving up their rights, even if such an action would result in what they know would be the betterment of the community. It is the same mentality that prevailed in Eden: we have a right to do what we want. We should be able to learn from that example that part of man's sinful nature is to demand his rights and will, even over God's. Man will not yield his rights. There's one thing people like even less than yielding their rights: having their rights **taken** from them. Consequently, a group of picketers is up against quite a problem.

What such militant disciples often fail to recognize is that people will yield their rights only when they become Christians. When a person is a Christian, yielding his rights is (or should be) part of business-as-usual due to the Lordship of Christ in his life. However, until such time as that, people will fight tooth and nail for their rights. That's where our picketers come in. More often than not, they aren't trying to make disciples by their picketing. They're just fighting for their rights.

WHERE TO DRAW THAT LINE...

If, in spite of all I've said to this point, you are determined to cling to your picket sign and fight off all the ills of society by using physical means, where are you going to draw the line? Abortion is a terrible sin worthy of any picketer's time, but it isn't the only sin going.

I am aware of a great number of others, and I'd like something done about these. I think we should close all the taverns. I also think we should have all the movie theaters shut down. If you're like most people, you're probably saying, "I don't see anything wrong with that. I see nothing wrong with movies." This presents us with a problem. Who is right about which activities are the worst and need our protest? Since everybody has his own idea about which sin is the worst, where do we draw the line?

I submit to you that there is no place where we can draw the line if we're going to engage in a physical battle. You may wish to draw the line at abortion clinics, saying, "We'll picket abortion clinics, and that's all. We'll go no further. After all, abortion is the murder of innocent unborn children. What could be worse?"

Just about that time, somebody else will speak up about the evils of alcoholism. It breaks up families, often scarring children for life. These children will have to live their whole lives suffering with the emotional and psychological damage caused by it. At least aborted babies died quickly, spared a lifetime of suffering. It would then be somebody's consensus that alcoholism must be the worst sin.

But wait! Somebody else has an opinion! The local filling station is selling gas to non-Christians. Suppose that one of those non-Christians buying gas there goes out, gets drunk and kills somebody, possibly an innocent pregnant woman! That's even worse than abortion. Perhaps it's most important to picket and boycott gas stations! But there's a problem with that. If we start boycotting the gas stations because they sell gasoline to non-Christians, we won't have enough gas in our own tanks to drive to the next place we're going to picket.

ABORTION

One of the greatest crusades in the Church today is the fight against legalized abortion. Unquestionably, it is a great tragedy. Yet, I don't believe that God is as concerned as we are about having a law passed to prohibit abortion. Don't misunderstand me to be saying that abortion is a joy and delight. I believe it is a tragedy. I just think that most Christians are upset about the wrong thing.

The tragedy of abortion is not the babies who die. According to the Bible those babies are going to heaven. If you accept that, why would babies' going to heaven bother God? If God were vehemently opposed to babies' being in heaven, He would never allow crib death. No, there is no tragedy in babies' going to heaven. The tragedy of abortion is the heart of the mother.

Mothers' hearts have grown so cold and hard that these women can go through an abortion without even blinking an eye. The love of a mother for her child is the most natural thing in the world, yet that response is no longer found in many mothers today. Surely this is the true tragedy. God's greatest concern is not about dead bodies, but about live bodies in which souls reside that do not know Him.

As sad as it may sound, abortion may well be God's answer to the **prayerlessness** of the Church today. Millions of people have gone to heaven through abortion. Perhaps more people have gone to heaven through abortion than through the prayer and evangelism of the Church.

If you are crusading against abortion, why are you

doing it? Is your goal simply to have our federal and state laws changed? What does that accomplish for God? If we have abortion abolished without turning any hearts toward God, then those babies who are now going to heaven will probably be born into ungodly homes and, considering how little the Church engages in prayer and evangelism, will spend eternity in hell.

Today's abortion epidemic may well be a sign to a prayerless Church that we have aborted the work of God through our complacency in seeking Him. This is by no means an indictment against the Crisis Pregnancy Centers or against others who are trying to prevent abortion. I believe they have helped many people. However, I do maintain that prayer is the chief thing, the first thing and the most important thing we can do. We will find ourselves in a very serious predicament if we neglect it in favor of physical activities.

CIVIL DISOBEDIENCE

A minister friend of mine had decided to further his education at a secular university. In his philosophy class, the professor brought up the issue of Christians' practicing civil disobedience. He said that even Jesus practiced civil disobedience by constantly opposing the system of the day. After listening to this long enough, my friend made a comment that changed the professor's views. He said, "The only real law at that time in Palestine was the law of the Roman Empire. Jesus never once opposed that government. He even admonished people to pay taxes to the Empire, to render to Caesar the things that are Caesar's. His only opposition was against the wicked religious organization that thrived in Israel in the name of God."

The Church needs to be very clear about Christianity's relationship to civil disobedience as much as that university professor. Believers today justify their disobedience to governmental authority by claiming the same kinds of things that professor did. They say civil disobedience has biblical precedent, citing Acts 5 and Daniel 3, the only two episodes in the Bible which even remotely resemble civil disobedience. However, in those instances, godly men were disobeying evil rulers who were imposing their morals on them by demanding that they renounce their God. But abortion is not being imposed on us. Nobody is being forced to have an abortion. Therefore we are standing in opposition to our Lord's teaching by disobeying those in authority. I agree that the morals of men could sink so low that abortion could become mandatory some day. That is why we must desperately seek God concerning this today. However, for Christians to obstruct law enforcement by opposing a law that is not imposed on them is not only civil disobedience, but disobedience to God as well.

PERSECUTION FOR THE SAKE OF WHAT?

Since the Church has decided to fight a physical battle, attempting to force the world to give up its rights, the Church has come under a great deal of persecution. Many cheerfully acknowledge this on the grounds that if the Church is doing Her job, She should be persecuted to some extent. They add that Jesus said that those who are persecuted are blessed. However, there's a little more to what Jesus said than just that.

"Blessed are those who are persecuted because of righteousness, for theirs is the kingdom of heaven. Blessed are you when people insult you, persecute you and falsely say all kinds of evil against you because of me. Rejoice and be glad, because great is your reward in heaven, for in the same way they persecuted the prophets who were before you. You are the salt of the earth. But if the salt loses its saltiness, how can it be made salty again? It is no longer good for anything, except to be thrown out and trampled by men" (Matt. 5:10-13).

Jesus wasn't encouraging a persecution complex. We

could go into the locker room of the Chicago Bears, sound a cheer for the Green Bay Packers, and get persecuted for it. Yet, we wouldn't be particularly blessed for that. Jesus spoke of being persecuted **for the sake of righteousness and on account of Him**. Yet, today, I fear the Church is being persecuted for things that do not fall into these honorable categories. Contrary to popular opinion, persecution for the sake of righteousness and for Christ's sake have nothing to do with our outward actions. Being persecuted for righteousness has everything to do with people's seeing Christ in us.

I recall once gracing a "Christian" home with the dubious honor of an unannounced visit. En route to the living room I passed by the kitchen. As I did so, I noticed many empty beer cans and other paraphernalia. After speaking briefly to the people I came to visit, I left. On my way out, though, I noticed that all the evidence of the party had been cleaned up. I didn't have to conduct myself that way. I could have made a big enough fuss that they would have thrown me out. Keeping with today's thinking, I could then proudly say, "I have been persecuted for the sake of righteousness." That would have had nothing to do with righteousness. I just would have been bringing persecution down upon myself.

In Matthew, chapter five, Jesus also spoke about our being the salt of the earth. He said that we are the salt of the earth, but that if we have lost our savor we are good for nothing. There is one Greek word for our equivalent phrase, "lost its savor." This Greek word implies the quality of being insipid, unable to stimulate. One of the characteristics of salt is that it stimulates thirst. We, as the salt of the earth, should be causing others to thirst for what we have. However, if we lose that quality, we are good for nothing but to be trodden under the feet of men.

For the most part, what we call "being persecuted for the sake of righteousness" has more to do with being insipid than it does with being righteous. We have lost our savor;

people do not thirst for what we have. Therefore, we are being trodden under the feet of men.

We live in a world where more people than ever before call themselves Christian, and, yet, the Church is more threatened today than She has been in a long time. Why is that? Because we have decided to fight a physical battle against the results of sin instead of battling the cause of sin by changing the hearts of men.

Do you really want to be effective in changing this world? I believe that most Christians who campaign and picket want nothing more than to do this. Certainly, attempting to change this sinful world is the right thing to do. However, protesting and lobbying is an exercise in doing the right thing the wrong way. If we really wish to have a lasting, significant impact on this world, **we must first seek God**. Pray, pray, and pray. Then, go out with the anointing of God on your life and draw people to Christ. Develop through prayer that quality of life that causes others to thirst. Restore the savor to the salt and the power to the gospel.

Remember that laws are for the lawless, not for law-abiders. Abortion could be legal and it wouldn't hurt a thing if everyone were a Christian. The legal drinking age could be twelve and it wouldn't hurt our society at all if we all followed Christian principles. Changing the law does not affect our hearts. Changing our hearts **does** affect our laws.

CHAPTER ELEVEN

DILIGENTLY SEEKING GOD

> "Our praying needs to be pressed and pursued with an energy that never tires, a persistency which will not be denied, and a courage, which never fails."
> —E.M. Bounds

When I was a boy, one of my favorite stories was "Aladdin and the Magic Lamp" from the *Tales of the Arabian Nights*. On a rainy day, I could read it time and again and still get the same thrill out of it. I think we all know the story about the boy who found the magic lamp in which a genie resided. The genie granted Aladdin three wishes, and the rest is history. What baffled me was the lack of any real relationship between Aladdin and the genie. I thought it would be neat to have a genie as a friend, but Aladdin and the genie never socialized and never really developed a friendship. Their only communication was initiated by Aladdin when he was in a tight spot and needed something. He was interested only in getting as much as he could out of the genie. He appeared sort of selfish and insensitive to me—even as a boy.

Yet many of us Christians are guilty of the same selfishness and insensitivity. Tragically, we treat our God and Father like a genie in a magic lamp. Like Aladdin with his genie in the little story, we often have no "social" relationship with our God. We call on Him only when we're in a tight spot and need something.

So many of us are seeking **things** from God under the pretense of seeking God. When we are sick, we seek healing from God. When hard financial times hit, we seek money from God. We call this seeking Him, but this is really light years from truly seeking Him. **The one who truly seeks God expects only one thing: God!** He is looking for God, not just the things God can give him. The prayer of his life is, "God, I just want You." When was the last time you prayed that prayer? I believe God wants to reveal Himself to us, but most of us just aren't interested.

It has always been my contention that we share a common trait with God in relationships. Anytime we begin a new relationship we are hesitant to reveal very much about who we really are. However, if that relationship begins to develop and we recognize that this person is truly interested in who we are, we begin to tell this person things about ourselves that we would tell no one else. In the same way, God is hesitant to reveal very much of Himself to any casual seeker who can "take it or leave it." However, when a person is truly interested in seeing who He is, he will seek Him in prayer. To such a person, God will reveal Himself in dynamic ways.

CRISIS PRAY-ERS

One of the greatest weaknesses of Christians today is

caused by our undue concern with the affairs of this world. Frequently, our jobs demand so much from us that there is no time left for God. Other times, our social lives, that football game or TV show we can't miss, or our hobbies devour our time. We fold our arms, raise our eyebrows, and sigh, "It's not my fault I'm not praying. There just aren't enough hours in the day." But when one of our children is seriously ill, or we receive a salary cut at work, or are diagnosed as terminally ill, the day seems to expand. Suddenly, there's time enough to pray. When things get bad enough, we pray. We are then what I call "crisis pray-ers," a people with sporadic prayer lives, bouncing from crisis to crisis.

If we only pray when we are in the midst of crisis, we develop the idea that prayer is just an "SOS" to God. Consequently, we never pray unless there is a disaster so great that we need to transmit a distress call to God. We're left with the misconception that prayer is a communication used exclusively as a remedy to overwhelming tragedy.

Not only does this limit the amount of time we pray, it hurts the quality of our prayers as well. During tragedy we focus our prayers on the urgent and tend to ignore the important. It may be **urgent** that we receive a sum of money, that we or someone we know receives a healing, but it is very, very **important** to just sit back and tell God how much we love and need Him. During a crisis, praying an "important" prayer is difficult. That's why we need to pray in non-crisis (In fact, we must!). If the only time we pray, is during a crisis, there's something wrong.

CRISIS-PRODUCED PRAYER MEETINGS

One day, my dad, who worked with my mom at a Bible college, telephoned me to tell me about a tremendous financial problem threatening the school. The need was so urgent that a special series of faculty-student prayer meetings was called. As my dad was telling me about this, the Holy

Spirit impressed me with a thought: "What will happen to these prayer meetings as soon as God honors their prayers by meeting their need?"

The same thing seems to happen all the time. We call prayer meetings when we're in a jam. God meets our need. We call off the prayer meetings because we're no longer in a jam. This demonstrates a point that seems quite ironic to me. Our primary goal is to resolve our conflict and we use prayer as a means to achieve this goal. God's goal, on the other hand, is to see us pray, and He takes advantage of our conflicts to achieve that goal. Our big concern is getting our needs met, but that is very insignificant on our Father's scale of interest. He is most concerned about our praying.

These transitory crisis prayer meetings are a reflection of ailing individual prayer lives. If prayer is not a regular part of our lives, we often feel the need for special prayer meetings. If prayer **is** a regular part of our lives, when a special need arises, it will simply slide into our ongoing prayers. Such a lifestyle of prayer will stand fast because it is based on a commitment to a life of prayer. But these special prayer meetings will always be transitory because they are based on commitment to a crisis. When the crisis ends, the prayer meetings will always end with it.

There is another reason why crisis pray-ers quit praying as soon as their crisis passes: they are just plain exhausted. Crisis praying is very hard on a person simply because of the tremendous tension and stress the crisis has caused. But when we pray only during a crisis, we assume that prayer is always that exhausting. Most think, "Why, prayer is simply too hard to engage in every day!" However, that notion can't be right because Jesus said, "...my burden is light" (Matt. 11:30). The only way to exchange our heavy burden for His light one is to make prayer a daily practice.

Crisis pray-er, consider what would happen in your life if after the next crisis you continued to pray in the same way you did during the crisis. I believe you could experience the abundant life Jesus came to bring you. You would not only see God answer your prayer by removing and resolving your crisis, but every day you would be investing precious time in His presence which would work to keep you from the next crisis!

A LIFESTYLE OF SEEKING GOD

Dick Eastman's "Change the World School of Prayer" challenged me to develop a regular prayer life. Dick spent two days at our church teaching this seminar on the importance of prayer. By the conclusion of that second day, I was determined to invest my life in really seeking God.

After about two months of spending one or two hours praying each day, I found myself boasting to God about how well I was doing. I beamed, "God, I'm diligently seeking You now." God pulled the proverbial rug out from under my feet, though, by speaking to my heart: "Ron," He said, "you're just beginning." Before He brought me to that place, I was so far out of touch with Him that I could never have heard Him.

Diligently seeking God is more than what we do during our prayer time. Seeking God becomes a lifestyle. It becomes a mind-set that permeates all activities of life. It grows into a passionate, all-consuming trek, searching after the One in Whose hands the fate of the universe lies. It is this drive that leads us to make (not find) time for God. One who is seeking God doesn't do it in his spare time, when there's nothing else to do.

OAK TREES DON'T GROW OVER NIGHT

We live in an age of instant pudding, instant milk, instant cereal, and a host of other "instant" food products. To speed up the heating of the instant food that requires cooking, we even have microwave ovens. Then because we don't have very much time between the moment we put our food in the oven and take it out, we have remote control devices that allow us to operate our living room TV sets from the kitchen. We are an instant people living in an instant world, and this sometimes affects our faith.

Often we go to the altar to pray, but if God can't compete with our microwave's most recent speed record, we give up and seek to answer the prayer ourselves, proclaiming it as a step of faith. But sometimes it simply takes time, and we have to be willing to take a real step of faith: trusting God and waiting for Him to answer.

This is also true when we're seeking God not just for things, but for who He is. It takes time. There's no quick, easy short cut. If it didn't take time, this seeking God I speak of could hardly be described as diligent.

Rev. Don Meyer, a teacher I had in Bible college, was forever fond of saying, "Oak trees don't grow over night, but weeds do." The more I grow in the Lord, the more I see the truth of that statement.

WHAT GOD DOESN'T KNOW CAN'T HURT US

Worship is a tremendously important part of seeking God. The Lord inhabits the praise of His people, so it's fair to say that worship generates the presence of God. That's one reason why those who want God have a tendency to worship God more than those who don't. It's these people who want to be in His presence, where they can get to know Him. If a believer fails to worship regularly, he develops a very cold heart and drifts very far from his God. This is also true of churches that tend to downplay worship collectively. Those churches tend to become very stale and very distant from God. We who wish to seek God must lift our hearts and voices in united praise and adoration to our God.

"Yet a time is coming and has now come when the true worshipers will worship the Father in spirit and truth, for they are the kind of worshipers the Father seeks. God is spirit, and his worshipers must worship in spirit and truth" (John 4:23,24).

Jesus said that God is **seeking** worshipers. That means He's not indifferent about it. He's not sitting around nonchalantly waiting for worshipers. He's seeking them! That in and of itself constitutes a call to worship as far as we are concerned. Moreover, God is not seeking just any kind of worshipers. He is seeking true worshipers, those who will worship Him in spirit and truth. If we are going to seek God, we must worship Him. Yet, in the Church today our worship is particularly weak in that last category: truth.

In Psalm 51:3, David acknowledges his sin saying, "...my sin is always before me." Like David, we feel that our sin stands out like a sore thumb. Whenever we go to prayer, the first thing that comes to mind is what rotten villains we are in comparison to Jesus and how we have fallen short of the glory of God. We are often bitter or afraid to trust God, yet won't admit it to Him. We worship under false pretense, assuming that what God doesn't know can't hurt us.

Did you know that we can never surprise God? Some Christians have the idea that if they were to be really candid with the Lord about who and what they are, He would be shocked! However, I just can't imagine God's standing in heaven with His mouth hanging open and His hands set firmly on His hips saying, "I didn't know that about you!" He already knew all about us. We can't surprise Him or fool Him.

Therefore, God won't think less of us if we talk to Him about our bad temper, our lust, our fear, our jealousy, or our bitterness. He already knows all about it and is waiting for us to come to Him with the problem. When we go to God in truth, then God can work in our life. I'm not saying that He is unable to work in our life if we don't go to Him in truth. He always has the ability to work in any "hidden" area of our lives. The real problem is that when we are trying to hide something from Him, we won't accept that help He is always able to provide. To accept His help, we must admit we have a problem.

"SEARCH ME, O GOD"

If we truly want God, we must open our heart to God and give Him free reign in every aspect of our life. There can be no areas of our life that we're "not going to bother God with."

"Search me, O God, and know my heart; test me and know my anxious thoughts" (Ps. 139:23).

That verse is a daily part of my life. It's not something I do once and for all. I must daily pray and open my heart to my Father. Unfortunately most Christians don't do this. They won't open their whole heart. Instead they present God with a *Reader's Digest* version. They open selected portions of their heart and no more. Some refuse to ask God to search their heart and check their motives.

Others refuse to open their heart and bring their own problems to God in prayer, but they bring the problems of others to Him. I have met self-proclaimed prayer warriors who claim to spend many hours in prayer daily, and, yet, their lives are packed with all types of problems: family problems, church problems, personal problems, and the list goes on and on. These are results of an unbalanced prayer life. Anybody can spend time with God (even if he has to force himself to do it!), but those who are really developing their relationship with God are those who are asking God to look into their own heart. These people aren't spending all their time asking God to take care of other people's problems. They are letting God take care of their problems as well. They are an open book to the Lord. They're allowing God to search their heart from ceiling to cellar.

As God searches our hearts, He brings to our attention hindrances in our relationship with Him. It is absolutely crucial that these hindrances be eliminated, or else we will never have a ministry of intercessory prayer which is operating at maximum efficiency. The more we allow God to thus transform us into the image of His Son, the more powerful our prayers will become.

"TEST ME..."

The second part of Psalms 139:23 says, "...test me and know my anxious thoughts." The phrase "anxious thoughts" can be translated "desires" in this text. It's important to realize that desire is more than a simple wish. It is a deep-seated craving, an intense longing. This sheds new light on this verse. The Psalmist is essentially saying, "God, look into my heart and know the things that are deep-seated longings. Put me to the test on these desires. I will pay any price to have these desires fulfilled."

When we desperately want something with all of our being, we're ready to pay any price to get it. You may have had a very strong desire that led you to pay whatever price was required to obtain it. That was the position of the Psalmist. He was consumed with a longing, but not for a house or something material. He was obsessed with a longing for God, and he was telling God he'd pay whatever price was required to satisfy that longing.

In his classic, *The Necessity of Prayer*, E.M. Bounds writes that desire goes before prayer. Desire gradually builds until it breaks forth into prayer. Desire is silent; prayer is the verbal expression of the desire of our hearts. Our failure to pray stems from our lack of desire for God. We've reached a sort of passive indifference in which we profess our love for God, but deep down in our hearts we have no burning desire for Him.

Despite the absence of this desire, the Church is involved in prayer. Things! As I mentioned earlier, we seek things from God, usually when we're in a crisis. But prayer prompted by things is transitory at best. We quit praying when we get the thing we want. On the other hand, prayer that is prompted by great longing for God leads us into regular, continual prayer.

Why do you think we have developed so much theology on faith today? We have found that if we properly exercise faith, we can obtain the thing we want without having to spend much time at it. Subsequently, we are saying today that if we pray more than once about something, we show it is a lack of faith. This theology is born out of a thing-seeking society. Such theology effectively prevents us from really knowing our God. Under that theology we could only pray, "God, I want to know You" once. Supposedly, to pray that prayer more would indicate a lack of faith. But the fact is, to know God, we must spend time seeking Him. That takes more than one little "faith" prayer.

"LORD, HOW LONG?"

It's not uncommon to ask the question, "How long, Lord, am I going to have to pray and seek You?"

Bill Gothard once shared a story from his childhood that answered this question. Bill and his brother shared a room while they were growing up. While Bill was very neat, his brother was very messy. Half the room looked like a museum, and the other half looked like the site of a Civil War battle. This bothered Bill, so he decided to make his brother's bed every morning to show him how much he loved him (also hoping his brother would start making his own bed). After doing this for several weeks with no response from his brother, Bill was a bit discouraged and went to talk to God about it. He asked the Lord how long he would have to make his brother's bed. God answered him with a question: "Why are you making his bed?" Bill replied, "Because I love him." God, in turn, said, "How long do you intend to love him?"

How long are we going to pray and seek God? We can answer this question by determining how long we intend to love Him. The degree to which we love and want God will determine the time factor in prayer.

It's time to stop seeking things and start seeking God. It's time to stop seeking the gift and, instead, seek the Giver. Once we have God, we have all that He possesses.

CHAPTER TWELVE

COMMUNICATING LIKE CHRIST

> "Until self-effacing men return again to spiritual leadership, we may expect a progressive deterioration in the quality of popular Christianity year after year until we reach the point where the grieved Holy Spirit withdraws like the Shekinah from the temple."
> —Dr. A.W. Tozer

Do you remember the last time you delivered a sermon or a Sunday school lesson that packed all the power of a Sominex tablet? Have you ever reached the point where you just don't have anything worthwhile to teach or preach about? Thomas Paine was wrong; it's time like **these** that try men's souls.

Such times leave you frustrated thinking, "Why can't I be more like Christ?" He never puts anyone to sleep. The fact of the matter is that when Jesus Christ spoke, everybody listened. He spoke with such authority that prostitutes and tax collectors even ended up praising God! What's more He even got through to the stuck-up, know-it-all pharisees. He was so effective that they were so convicted that, upon rejecting His words, they couldn't stand to hear anymore and set out to stone Him on several occasions.

If you can relate to this, I have good news for you. You **can** be more like Christ. In light of this, I'm going to rephrase your question so that it asks, "Why am I not more like Christ?" In answer to **this** question, I feel compelled to answer, "You can't be more like Christ if you don't pray like He did." As we will soon see, prayer was the lifeblood of Jesus Christ's ministry.

AUTHORITY

One of the most potent qualities of Jesus' preaching and teaching was the authority with which He spoke. "The people were amazed at his teaching, because he taught them as one who had authority, not as the teachers of the law" (Mark 1:22).

Today, many people do not understand what is meant by "authority" in this context. Although we hear much about the authority of the believer in terms of the power we may exercise over demons, we hear little about the kind of authority referred to in Mark 1:22. To even begin to understand this concept, one must first acknowledge that authority of this kind is granted because of one's position, not because of his vocal power. Since we are in Christ (that is our position), we have authority. One man's ability to project his voice farther than another man does not give him greater authority.

Christians have frequently mistaken the physical manifestation of man's voice as authority. Pentecostals are particularly notorious for this. In prayer, for example, if we are required to pray for something a second time, we will do so, only more loudly than the first time. If we are required to pray a third time, we will shout. Apparently, we have reasoned that the increased volume of our prayers will in some way serve the devil with a spiritual eviction notice, forcing him to leave. But, of course, this is erroneous. It is our authority in Christ that forces him out, not our loud voices.

I became a victim of this misconception while I was teaching a prayer seminar. After the first evening sessions, the pastor and I went out to a local restaurant for a cup of coffee. During the course of our conversation, the pastor complimented me saying, "This is perhaps the finest teaching on prayer my church has ever heard. But if you don't start shouting and pacing back and forth on the platform, my people simply will not believe a word you say." Despite his warning, I continued the seminar as usual, refusing to become someone I am not to accommodate these people. As the pastor warned, those people didn't believe a word I said. In fact, anyone who is familiar with my preaching style must realize by now that I left that church with the congregation absolutely convinced that I should have become a plumber or anything else but a preacher.

That church was under the impression that authority was the result of a series of physical actions. It seems that if I had employed some cheap theatrics to meet that church's criteria for authority, they would have wholeheartedly accepted my message. However, because I did not, that congregation assumed that I had nothing valid to say.

What, then, is authority? Webster defines it as, "the ability to influence or command thought." As Christians (and especially ministers!) we are in the business of influencing thought as we are constantly endeavoring to convince people of our beliefs. Any man who is successful at convincing people of his beliefs is considered an authority.

In forming our concept of authority, we should also consider the Greek word *exousia* for which we render the English word "authority" in Mark 1:22 and elsewhere in the

New Testament. *Exousia* implies power and knowledge. In other words, we find that the person who understands authority (because of his position) can exercise his ability to influence or command thought based on his knowledge of the power available to him.

Because we are in Christ, we have authority. We will struggle with exercising this authority until we fully understand the power available to us. It is this power which is one of the two basic means through which authority is realized. The second is knowledge. "Jesus replied, 'You are in error because you do not know the Scriptures or the power of God'" (Matt. 22:29).

Jesus knew what was wrong with the religious leaders in Jerusalem: they didn't really know the Scriptures, nor did they know anything about the power of God. This prevented them from being sincere people of God and also kept them from being good teachers. Jesus indicated here that it is necessary for a teacher to have a knowledge of the Scriptures and of the power of God. That sort of teacher will influence thought.

AUTHORITY THROUGH KNOWLEDGE

"Stop listening to instruction, my son, and you will stray from the words of knowledge" (Prov. 19:27). In this verse, presumably written by King Solomon, the word "instruction" is an English translation of the Hebrew word *musar*. *Musar* connotes chastisement and self-denial. In our contemporary colleges and universities, *musar* plays a significant role. Ask any conscientious college student, and he'll tell you that self-denial is a necessary element of his academic life.

Self-denial walks hand-in-hand with discipline, an endangered species in our self-indulgent culture. However, those few who dare to be disciplined in any given area find that they become very knowledgeable in that area. For example, my father, who has been an automobile mechanic all his life, became knowledgeable about cars because he invested years of his life disciplining himself to study them and work on them.

As Christians, we need to practice self-denial and discipline every bit as much as scholars and skilled workers. That self-denial and discipline needs to come in the form of prayer and the study of God's Word. These disciplines yield knowledge, just as the others do. But instead of yielding knowledge about automobiles or calculus as the others do, these yield knowledge of God. God's Word provides us with a knowledge **about** God, while prayer will help us **know** God.

If we study God's Word, we will continually run into this one command: pray! If we study God's Word and yet don't pray, then we have "strayed from the words of knowledge by not listening to *musar* (discipline/instruction)." It is apathy toward this biblical admonition to pray that has brought us preachers who can quote God's Word in Hebrew and Greek, but can't teach or preach their way out of a paper bag. They may even preach with great eloquence and fabulous style, but neither their eloquence nor their style will change lives. They are talented speakers, but powerless preachers. How could they be any different? Without prayer, they are cutting themselves off from one of authority's two constituents (i.e., knowledge).

"My son, if you accept my words and store up my commands within you, turning your ear to wisdom and applying your heart to understanding, and if you call out for insight and cry aloud for understanding, and if you look for it as for silver and search for it as for hidden treasure, then you will understand the fear of the Lord and find the knowledge of God" (Prov. 2:1-5).

This segment of Proverbs 2 shows us the importance of the combination of the Word of God and prayer. Practicing these two elements will result in the knowledge of God. Therefore, I must discipline myself to be in prayer and the Word of God, for then only will I know God.

AUTHORITY THROUGH POWER

"Now to him who is able to do immeasurably more than all we ask or imagine, according to his power that is at work within us" (Eph. 3:20).

Paul the apostle had a healthy understanding of God's omnipotence. He understood that God is able to do anything. At times we have problems that seem as if they are going to sweep over us and drown us. We don't know how they can ever be solved. Yet, the worst of them all is mere child's play for God. There is nothing He is unable to do. Yet, if this is the case, why do we not see more miracles?

Our text from Paul's letter to the church in Ephesus explains why: because God only does things in accordance with the power at work in us. If that power is vibrantly flowing through us, we will see great signs and wonders. If, on the other hand, there is no power at work in us, we will see only what the hand of man can accomplish. Our lack of miracles is nothing less than a consequence of our spiritual power shortage. We simply do not have the necessary power at work in us, and the only one we can get the power from is God. We can receive that power only in prayer.

In Jeremiah 33:3, "the weeping prophet," as he is known, quotes the Lord as saying, "Call to me and I will answer you and tell you great and unsearchable things you do not know." This is quite simple in theory, but very difficult in practice. God has promised us those great and mighty things if only we'll call to Him. When we are communing with Him, we develop an awareness of His power. The more time I spend with Him, the more I sense His power.

It is important to realize that in prayer, God's power becomes a reality in our lives, not just a theology. A correct theology about God's power tells me only that God gives me power as His own. However, I will not see and experience that power until I transfer my head knowledge about God's power into heart knowledge via prayer. After prayer, my intellectual assent blossoms into a life-changing reality which will permeate my life and ministry.

All believers have this power available to them, but only those who pray are generating that power. The apostle James spoke of this power when he stated, "The prayer of a righteous man is powerful and effective" (James 5:16). There is one Greek word which we render as the two English words "effectual" and "fervent." This word, *energeo*, denotes the involvement of energy. Consequently, we could interpret this passage, "...the energized prayer of a righteous man is powerful and effective."

I believe prayer and its interaction with our faith can be likened to a power generator. Where an earthly generator is concerned, the amount of power generated is increased by turning the handle in a designated direction. The more the handle is turned, the more power the generator puts out. Where our "faith generator" is concerned, we increase the power of our faith by turning a handle called "prayer." Prayer is a faith-builder. The more we pray, the more our faith is built up.

This is corroborated in Hebrews 12:2 where the writer admonishes his readers to run the spiritual race: " Let us fix our eyes on Jesus, the author and perfecter of our faith." Looking to Jesus, as we do in prayer, builds our faith.

BUILDING COMPASSION

"When he saw the crowds, he had compassion on them, because they were harassed and helpless, like sheep without a shepherd" (Matt. 9:36). Throughout His life and earthly ministry, Jesus was a man of deep, limitless love. The compassion He continually exhibited toward others was a byproduct of that love. When He taught the crowds in those arid lands, He empathized with them, grieving with them in their pain. To Him, those people were not just automatons, nameless, faceless people. No, instead, He saw them as real people with real hurts. He observed them as tragic examples of man without God.

Today, however, many teachers and preachers have no compassion for their crowds and multitudes. They look at them just as an audience. Their primary concern is putting on a performance. But this is not Jesus' way. If we are to be Christ-like in our communicating, we must be people who have compassion for those who hear us.

The apostle John wrote, "Whoever does not love does not know God, because God is love" (1 John 4:8). This presents us with a problem. It seems that we cannot even pray for love. I often hear people praying for love, but I believe they are praying in error. Nowhere in the Bible are we commanded or even urged to pray for love. That is because love is very unique. God will not simply bestow love upon a person just because he asks for it. I don't believe that God will ever just plunk down love upon a person in bulk quantities. It simply doesn't work that way. You see, if a person does not love, his lack of love is just a symptom of a much more serious problem documented in the aforementioned verse: he does not know God.

Today's saints do not need more love. What we really need is more of God. When we have love, it is because we have God. When we do not have love, it is just a side-effect of our own distance from God. That is why the Lord will not answer a petition for love. If He were to just inject a person with love somehow, He would not be dealing with that person's real problem (i.e., estrangement from his Creator). This lack of love can be dealt with only after a person realizes that he needs more of God, that he needs to truly know his God.

The best and only way I know of to get to know God is to dare to spend time with Him. As we do this, we begin to sense His presence, and, subsequently, His character. As we pray consistently, that character rubs off on us until we are completely covered and filled up with it, and chief among the attributes of that character is love. From personal experience, I can state that once I'm filled with the Lord and His character, I don't have any trouble loving even my worst enemy. However, if I stayed out of God's presence long enough, I would struggle with loving anybody—given even the slightest provocation.

Compassion has been and will always be crucial to the ministry because compassion creates a "steadfast spirit" within the teacher or preacher, or a "right" spirit, as the King James Version translates it. King David testified to this truth in Psalm 51:10 where he pled, "Create in me a pure heart, O God, and renew a steadfast [right] spirit within me."

When a person has a right spirit, he ministers with conviction rather than condemnation. As Dick Eastman once said, "Condemnation kills, but conviction cures." Conviction draws people to God, but condemnation drives them away. What's more, Romans 8:1 states that condemnation is not for the believer: "Therefore, there is now no condemnation for those who are in Christ Jesus." That doesn't promise us that we'll never have feelings of condemnation, but it does assure us that those feelings will not come from God. When God deals with us and our sin, He will use conviction, not condemnation. In this way, we will be drawn to Him and not driven from Him.

Teachers and preachers who pray will always exude compassion, as well as a right spirit. When they speak, their message will reach down deep into the spirits of their listeners. Their words will encourage their hearers to draw nearer to God because then God will send His holy conviction down. When God's conviction results, our words have tremendous potential to influence and change lives, but that will never happen aside from prayer. Without prayer, lives and hearts will never really be changed.

I have heard "men of God" say some powerful things, but with a wrong spirit. The only substantial result was condemnation. This is so because the power of the preacher is not in his diction or his vocabulary, but in his spirit. That is why men of prayer preach with a right, steadfast spirit and usher in conviction. The power of these men is their spirit, which is, in turn, a result of prayer. Unfortunately, many people today are impressed with words when their main concern should be a man's spirit, who that man really is inside. We minister to others through who we are in Christ. If a man fails to develop God's character, he has nothing to offer others.

What we know **about** Jesus is really of very little importance if we do not **know** Him. If we know Jesus, we minister to others through His spirit in us. It is a spirit of love and compassion, not hate and revilement. Without that spirit, a preacher may say the correct things, but if he has a wrong spirit, only condemnation and strife will result, and the message will not be received. That is why I have always maintained that if a man is preaching in a condemning way, if you sense a heavy weight of condemnation descending on you, then he is preaching on a subject he has studied, but does not really know in his spirit.

Jesus was a man of deep compassion. He ministered in compassion, and He healed because of His compassion. If we are ever to minister as Jesus did, we must be spending time in His presence.

BUILDING WISDOM

In correspondence with the believers in Corinth, the apostle Paul mentioned that Jesus had become wisdom for us (1 Cor. 1:30). Therefore, any examination of Jesus' preaching must include some commentary on His wisdom, another factor we must consider if we truly wish to communicate as effectively as Jesus did.

Wisdom is lauded as "supreme" in Proverbs 4:7. "Therefore, get wisdom," the verse concludes. The King James Version translates the verse a bit differently by calling wisdom "the principal thing." Nowhere in the Scriptures is anything else referred to as "the principal thing." In fact, throughout the Bible, those who have walked closely with the Lord have hailed wisdom as one of the most godly and most desirable of all attributes.

This "principal thing" is procured only through prayer, as James 1:5 explains: "If any of you lacks wisdom, he should ask God, who gives generously to all without finding fault, and it will be given to him." Prayer is often a pursuit of wisdom. We pray many times because we need direction, insight, and knowledge. In prayer, we receive wisdom because it draws us closer to God, the One to whom there are no mysteries, the Author of all knowledge and wisdom.

AN EXERCISE IN FOOLISHNESS

It has been observed, and rightly so, that "The fool says in his heart, 'There is no God'" (Ps. 14:1). The fool, then, has an excellent reason for not praying. The way he sees things, there's nobody to pray to, no one to hear and answer his prayers. It would be foolishness compounded for one to pray to a God he does not believe in.

If this is true, then logic dictates that the wise man, on the other hand, says in his heart, "There is a God." The wise man must pray. He knows in his heart that in prayer he can draw near to the God whose resources are endless, and whose creative capacity to intervene on behalf of man is limitless.

Who is the most foolish, then? Is it the fool who insists there is no God and does not pray? Or is it the "wise" man who knows that God does indeed exist and does not pray? For us to proclaim that there is a God while lacking a prayer life is to make ourselves out to be bigger fools than the most adamant atheist or the most vocal agnostic. How foolish we prove ourselves to be by not praying to the God we claim loves us and created us!

THE BEGINNING OF WISDOM

In Proverbs 2:2-3,5 we read, "Turning your ear to wisdom and applying your heart to understanding, and if you call out for insight and cry aloud for understanding...then you will understand the fear of the Lord..."

Why does fearing the Lord become important to us? Because the fear of the Lord is the beginning of wisdom. For many years, I have made the preceding portion of Scripture a part of my prayer life. I have asked God to give me the knowledge of Him and to help me understand the fear of the Lord.

The fear of the Lord is by no means a new idea, but it is, unfortunately, a rather abstract concept as far as many are concerned. I know that many believers today wonder just what this fear of the Lord is. Does it mean cowering in a corner somewhere for fear that God is going to bang us on the head with some kind of spiritual sledge hammer? Does it mean walking around in a state of paranoia for fear that the Lord has a contract out on our lives? To both questions, the answer is a definite, absolute "No!"

To fear God means to maintain an attitude of respect and reverence toward Him. He is our Creator; we must revere Him. He is our Father; we must honor Him. This inevitably leads us to obedience of His commands. It would be the height of disrespect to ignore His wishes. In accordance with our respect and honor for Him, we obey Him. This obedience further perpetuates prayer because we then obey God's command that we pray.

So it is that prayer becomes the active practice of fearing God. Without prayer, we cannot say that we fear God. Through prayer, the results of fearing God develop in our lives. For example, we begin to hate evil, pride, and arrogance (Prov. 8:13). It prolongs our lives (Prov. 10:27). It allows one to sleep satisfied, untouched by evil (Prov. 19:23). Furthermore, we are rewarded with riches, honor, and life (Prov. 22:4).

God teaches us the "fear of Him" as we sit patiently in His presence. Psalm 25:14 says, "The Lord confides in [reveals secrets to] those who fear him; he makes his covenant known to them." This is why the fear of the Lord is the beginning of wisdom—because prayer (the fear of the Lord) gets us God and God is wisdom. The secret of the Lord is for those who pray.

Wisdom enters the heart through prayer. While we are in prayer, God speaks to our hearts. The heart of the wise is the heart of the person of prayer. It becomes imperative for Christians to have a wise heart because wisdom helps us become better communicators.

The Book of Proverbs continues to shed light on our search for wisdom with 16:23 which declares, "A wise man's heart guides his mouth, and his lips promote instruction." The word instruction here means "persuasive." The verse could be paraphrased, "When the heart teaches a man's mouth to speak, his words become very persuasive."

This is the crux of the matter. We must be people of prayer so that wisdom will enter our hearts. Then the heart will teach the mouth to speak. When we speak from the heart, we are far more convincing than at any other time, and we are in the business of persuading people concerning the gospel. If I want to reach my maximum persuasiveness, I need to be spending as much time as possible in prayer.

THE FOUNDATION: FAITHFULNESS

There is an important foundation upon which all this must be built. That foundation is faithfulness, the important factor that figures in to make us effective to do the work of God. Contrast that to unfaithfulness. In Proverbs 22:12 it says, "The eyes of the Lord keep watch over knowledge, but he frustrates the words of the unfaithful." When the Bible makes such a general reference to faithfulness, it is referring to the pursuit of God (which, we have already found, is expressed through prayer). The end result of faithfulness in the spiritual realm is an intimacy with God. The faithful man, we must conclude, is, among other things, a man of prayer. Without prayer, there is no consistency in our pursuit of God.

The Scriptures indicate that the unfaithful man finds that his words are confused. Wisdom enters the heart through prayer. Without prayer, the heart does not teach the mouth to speak; therefore, our words become confused. There is an old proverb which tells us, "A message prepared in the intellect will only reach the intellect, but a message prepared in the heart will reach the heart."

If all we are trying to do is match wits with our audience, then we will never convince our listeners. I believe that the apostle Paul understood this. He was a highly-educated man, one who was considered an intellectual in his day. Yet, he did not awe his listeners with his impressive education or extensive vocabulary. Instead, he spoke from his heart. It was the heart of man that Paul wished to change, not the intellect.

Today, we are not in need of great analytical expositions of God's Word as much as we are in need of men who seek God. Too much preaching today is dull and unconvincing because it is being preached by men who spend no time with God.

King Solomon once remarked, "Many a man claims to have unfailing love, but a faithful man who can find?" (Prov. 20:6). Human nature hasn't changed much in all these centuries. Men are still fond of forever discussing their own virtues and their own sincerity. Yet, where are the men who are really faithful? Where are the people whose prime goal is to draw closer to God, which cannot be done without prayer? We need men and women who dare to pray without ceasing! At that point we can revisit the power of the gospel and come to people with a touch from God instead of just education and polish.

CHAPTER THIRTEEN

THE PRAYING CHURCH

> "The church that is not praying is playing."
> —Leonard Ravenhill

When my brother and I were teenagers, we were the original "odd couple." He was tall and muscular, and I was neither. He was very popular with all the girls. (Yes, at times it did seem as if he was popular with **all** the girls.) The only girls I was popular with were the girls who wanted to go out with my brother and saw me as a convenient way to reach their objective. I always played Jerry Lewis to his Dean Martin. Finally, I brought up the subject one day, asking him how I could generate a little more popularity with the fairer sex. He suggested that I lift weights as he had. I tried it, but it didn't work—after several days, nothing had changed.

In those early teen years, I didn't understand the importance of consistency. If I had continued working out in the gym for an extended period, I would have seen results. However, in the interim, I have come to appreciate the fact that consistency is the strength of any given endeavor, particularly prayer. Consistency in prayer is a real faith-builder.

When most of us get into a tight spot where were really need God, we realize then how inconsistent we really are in our Christian walk. Our faith is hindered and we reach a point of despair. What hinders our faith? Our own disobedience. The reverse is also true. Our obedience to God (particularly in prayer) builds our faith and we expect God to respond to our cries for help.

This principle works on the corporate level as well as on the individual level. If a church is consistent in prayer, that body will find that its faith in God has increased greatly. The kind of character qualities prayer builds in an individual, it also builds into the character of the praying church. That is why I believe it is so crucial to have some kind of daily prayer meeting in the church.

It is imperative today that we develop churches that pray, not just for answers that come through prayer, but for character development. In Galatians 6:9 we read, "Let us not become weary in doing good, for at the proper time we will reap a harvest if we do not give up." In prayer, we learn to "plow through" so that we can reap that harvest. The individual who prays learns more and more about tenacity as time goes on, and he will never give up.

I had traveled with Pray-Tell Ministries full-time for several years when I was asked to join the staff of a local church as minister of prayer. Though I had varied responsibilities, coordinating the prayer emphasis for the church was my greatest priority. The church has been "plowing through" in prayer for several years now and has been seeing God do exciting things. In the following pages, I will detail the prayer ministry of our church and supply some practical "how-to" tips on how to develop a praying church.

MORNING MANNA

Morning Manna (MM) is our daily prayer meeting which begins at 6:00 a.m. every Monday through Friday, concluding at 8:00 a.m. Those particular hours catch people on their way to work. It's a rare opportunity to attract a large number of men to prayer meetings, they are powerful assets.

The first half-hour is unstructured. From 6:00 until 6:30, people can come and spend time with God alone. Then from 6:30 to 7:30, an hour of structured prayer is offered, led by a different member of the pastoral staff every morning. The concluding half-hour is unstructured, as was the first.

We discovered that the most effective way to help people to pray at those early hours is to offer them a structural framework in which to work. I started MM in August of 1983. For the first three years, the full two hours were unstructured. The sanctuary was opened at 6:00 a.m., and people had the opportunity to come in and pray. We had a small group of stalwarts who came and lingered for five to fifteen minutes each day, but it scarcely grew for three years. In 1986, we decided to provide a more structured approach. The response was decidedly favorable. Attendance increased, with an average of ten to fifty people each day, and an all time high of seventy-five.

I received a little additional insight into our MM prayer meetings after visiting the Full Gospel Central Church in Seoul, Korea. While I was there, I noticed that Pastor Cho's church drew twenty thousand people to the morning prayer meeting. Twenty-thousand is only five percent of four hundred thousand. At that time, our church averaged fifty people at MM each morning. Also at that time, our church attendance averaged a thousand. Simple arithmetic shows us that our MM attendance was also five percent. So, five percent is a good goal to set.

REACHING FIVE PERCENT ATTENDANCE

No one wants to settle with just five percent of his church praying, but most of the time it's difficult to get even five percent praying. One thing seems to stand out above all other things in getting our church to pray: our senior pastor made it mandatory for his pastoral staff to attend. As we began to promote MM from the pulpit, sharing with our people that not only were we structuring it, but that the entire pastoral staff would be there, people began to respond. An old adage tells us, "As the pulpit goes, so goes the pew." I am convinced of this statement's truth. Further, I am certain that the involvement of our churches in prayer depends on our pastors' enthusiasm towards it and involvement in it.

Before the entire staff began joining in MM, I was periodically asked by those lay people attending, "Do the other pastors pray?" The average lay person assumes that his pastor is a person of prayer, but when he sees his pastor passing up opportunities to pray, he is confused. Pastors need to attend MM, if for no other reason, than to reassure and encourage his congregation. If they don't, they may conform to a plaque I once read which said, "There they go, so I must hasten to catch up with them and overtake them, for I am their leader."

Figure 1
MORNING MANNA FORMAT

A four-step approach to group prayer:

1. Songs of Praise and Worship — 10 minutes
2. Scripture Reading and confession — 10 minutes
   (read the Proverb of the day
3. Intercession — 30 minutes
4. Praying-in-the-harvest — 10 minutes

DETAILS OF FORMAT

#1. Songs and Worship. At 6:30, we begin the hour of structured prayer by calling everyone together into one area where we sing and worship together. This helps those who are not quite awake to wake up. It's important to be active, lest your MM group doze off like the apostles did in the garden. That's why we encourage audible worship, singing choruses that promote worship. We usually do this for approximately ten minutes.

#2. Scripture Reading and Confession. This second step offers each individual a time of introspection and, subsequently, confession. Soul-searching and confession are extremely important on a daily basis. Without them, ministries go bad and so do people because they are no longer asking God to check their motives. The leader explains that they are going to have a time of private confession and introspection. Then he reads a portion of Scripture, encouraging those gathered to let it speak to them.

When I lead MM groups, I read what I call "the proverb of the day." If it is the tenth day of the month, I read the tenth chapter of the Book of Proverbs. This not only brings the Word of God into the prayer time, but it also keeps one from dealing with the same sin over and over, causing the time to get stale and boring. When we take in God's Word, however, the Holy Spirit has a way of pointing out things we never give thought to. I encourage every MM group to allow the Word of God to be the finger of conviction and then admonish them to spend the next several minutes praying by themselves about how the Word spoke to them. Generally, we allocate about ten minutes to this step.

#3. Intercession. This is the largest single portion of time during the hour. This is a time set aside for praying for others. This is really the heart of the matter. This is where one has an opportunity to share prayer requests. Because of the importance of this step, I will deal with it in great detail later. On the average, we invest about thirty minutes in intercession.

Fugure 2
MORNING MANNA INTERCESSION SCHEDULE

Monday	City, State, Nation	1 Tim. 2:2
Tuesday	Families	Malachi 4:6
Wednesday	World Missions	Psalm 2:8
Thursday	Lost Souls, Revival	Psalm 85:6
Friday	Sunday's Services, Various Church Ministries	Eph. 5:18-21

#4. **Praying in the Harvest**. This is one of the most unique and also most powerful periods of prayer we have. At this time, we ask God to give us a harvest of souls from every direction of the community, spending time facing each of the four general directions and praying for them one at a time. Importantly, we do not pray to the north, south, east and west. Rather, we pray to God concerning each of them.

Rev. Larry Lea from Rockwell, Texas first introduced this creative means of prayer. It is based upon Isaiah 43:4-6: "Since you are precious and honored in my sight and because I love you, I will give men in exchange for you, and people in exchange for your life. Do not be afraid, for I am with you; I will bring your children from the east and gather you from the west. I will say to the north, 'Give them up!' and to the south, 'Do not hold them back!' Bring my sons from afar and my daughters from the ends of the earth.''

As I have already indicated, we stand and face each

direction as we pray for it. When a direction has been sufficiently prayed for, the leader instructs the group to change directions. This is done until all four directions have been prayed for. We do this because it gives us the opportunity to address the specific issues unique to each part of the community.

For instance, in Kenosha, when we pray toward the east, we are praying for the heart of the city, where the downtown area is located, as well as the ghetto. Meanwhile, most of our secondary schools are located in the north, so when we pray facing the north, we ask God to break the devil's grip over that area. Also, we each pray for individuals we know who live in a given direction.

This method of prayer has been very effective for us. We have literally prayed people into our church from every direction in the community. After praying this way for about ten minutes, we often conclude with a song of praise to cap the hour of structured prayer.

MORE ABOUT INTERCESSION

On each of the five days of the week, we have a different focus for intercession. We found it necessary to come up with a schedule to follow. Without it, there is too much repetition from one day to another. If there is no schedule, then the only other thing there is to do is to ask for prayer requests. There is certainly nothing wrong with asking for prayer requests, but if that's all we do, we usually have the same people every day with essentially the same request. That becomes a bit dull, hollow, and meaningless after a while. We found that having a determined focus for the day keeps things alive and provides a powerful vehicle for united prayer.

Monday: City, State, Nation. "...[Pray] for kings and all those in authority, that we may live peaceful and quiet lives in all godliness and holiness" (1 Tim. 2:2).

Every city has problems and every city has a governing

body. As we intercede on Monday mornings, we list all our prayer requests for our city on an overhead projector as individuals make them. Along with praying about a variety of issues, we always pray for our mayor. We follow the same procedure for the state and the nation, making sure that we pray for our state and nation. As soon as all the requests are listed on the overhead projector, the people are called to pray for the next half-hour, with the projector left on so that the group can refer back to it.

We have seen many exciting answers to prayer in our city. It was once suggested that we pray about the terrible grip alcohol has on our community, so we did. A few weeks later, as I was returning home after conducting a prayer seminar, I noticed that one of the most notorious bars in the city had burned to the ground. The bar used to cater to many young people who would later try to drive the country roads in an alcoholic stupor. We were all delighted to hear that the place was put out of commission—until two weeks later when a sign was erected on the bar property announcing the intended erection of a "bigger, better" bar, paid for with their compensation from their insurance company.

I realized that something different was going to have to happen if we were going to have an effect on the problem. I challenged our people to pray about the alcohol problem every Monday when they prayed for the city, state, and nation. Four months later, the following headline was emblazoned across the top of the front page of the local newspaper: "Times Are Tough For Tavern Keepers." The accompanying article went on to say, "Times are tough for local tavern keepers. And for many of them the future isn't much brighter. That's the story nationally. That's the picture locally." A local bar owner was interviewed, saying, "I wouldn't buy a tavern these days." The president of the Wisconsin Tavern League stated, "As many as twenty percent of the bars operating today will be out of business within five years."

We also prayed for our city's economy. The city is based

on blue collar industry, having an extremely high rate of unemployment, far beyond the national average. A year after we started praying for the economy, Wisconsin Power & Light decided to construct an industrial park in Kenosha County which, within the next decade, is expected to generate twenty thousand jobs.

Meanwhile, Chicago developers who own vacant land on the outskirts of Kenosha began saying that within the next ten years, they expected Kenosha to become the "hot spot" in our nation as far as employment is concerned. Can I allow our prayer group to take all the credit for this? I'm not sure. What I am sure of, though, is that things have happened exactly the way we prayed for them to happen.

Many of these things didn't happen until months after we had begun praying. I believe that this testifies to the importance of consistency. We didn't give up just because we didn't see results within the first days, weeks, or even months. But after we persevered, we began seeing tremendous results, perhaps greater than we had ever dared hope for.

Tuesday: Families. "He will turn the hearts of the fathers to their children, and the hearts of the children to their fathers..." (Mal. 4:6).

Broken homes are on the rise in our nation as never before. And recently, I have become aware of the situation as never before. One day I was in a city doing a prayer seminar when I noticed a car with a U-Haul trailer parked in front of a house. In front of the car was a young man in his twenties hugging what appeared to be a four-year-old boy. Both of them were sobbing, tears streaming down their cheeks. As the man attempted to stand, the little boy clung to him, trying to prevent him from leaving. It was certainly some kind of tearful farewell. And it was probably one exchanged between father and son. Just one of many thousands breaking the hearts of children and parents alike across our nation.

The singular purpose of Tuesday's intercession is to

turn the hearts of the fathers (i.e., parents) to the children. We pray for families in two ways:

1. Each person prays for his own immediate family first. Nothing touches the heart more than the home. It is also more easy to begin praying for your own family than for the family of someone else.

2. Then, the floor is open to prayer requests for families. I insist that only the initials be given for those couples who need prayer. This reduces the potential for gossip. After all, there is no need to give names and details. The Holy Spirit knows the situation intimately and can pray through us. The initials are written on the overhead projector and left up while our people go to prayer. After some time, everyone is asked to go on a prayer walk through the pews and pray for families who they know sit in the same general area each week.

Wednesday: World Missions. "Ask of me, and I will make the nations your inheritance, the ends of the earth your possession" (Ps. 2:8).

This is the day on which we intercede for our missionaries, also praying about other related world issues. Too many churches take no time to pray for their missionaries or the lost of the world. This approach works against this tendency. In this way, missionaries are prayed for each week, keeping their names fresh in the minds of the congregation.

For the most part, America is guilty of giving her money, but not her pray-ers to the missionary cause. We seem to depend on money more than anything else. In the New Testament, money and prayer are inseparable offerings in the Church. In Acts 10:31, an angel told Cornelius, "God has heard your prayer and remembered your gifts to the poor." Notice that both his alms and his prayer were remembered by God.

In many of the churches where MM is being held, we take the missionary plaques or cards and lay them on the table in the sanctuary. Then we instruct the people to go to the table and take one of the cards back to their place of prayer. After praying for one missionary they are free to get another card. Finally, we list some of the major missionary "hot spots' of the world and pray for them.

Thursday: Revival. "Will you not revive us again, that your people may rejoice in you?" (Ps. 85:6).

While attending the National Prayer Leaders Conference in Chicago, I found out some very interesting statistics concerning the historical relationship between prayer and revival in America. Comparisons were made between the rising number of prayer meetings being held in America today and the number of prayer meetings that were being held in the United Stated just before the great outpouring of the Holy Spirit at the turn of the last century. At that time in the late 1880s and early 1900s, hundreds of prayer meetings were being held in Washington, DC. Today over one thousand prayer meetings are being held in Washington, DC every week.

At the turn of the century, there was also a great stirring among ministers concerning their own need to pray. As I travel around the country I am seeing a similar interest. Pastors are becoming very concerned about their own prayer lives, but not for the same reasons as before. Church growth seems to be every pastor's buzz word. If you tell them prayer will make their church grow, they'll pray. In this current move towards prayer, pastors aren't just praying to make their churches grow; they are beginning to recall the very personal relationship they once had with God through prayer. They are realizing that their prayer lives have become consumed with nothing but the problems of the church. The are realizing that there's more to prayer than a quick means to church growth.

When we pray for revival, it has to be because God wants men reconciled with Himself, not just because we want a bigger church. A larger church will be the natural result of revival. The correct prayer is the one that cries out for the salvation of the lost, not the one that begs for church growth. Our motives must be the same as God's. God's motive is to glorify Himself. What is He most glorified by? Beautiful buildings or beautiful people?

In Kenosha, we have evangelism teams that go out each week to visit the people who have visited our church, or sometimes just to tell strangers about the good news. Their statistics showed that from the time we started praying for them in MM, the percentage of people who asked Christ into their lives increased by fifty percent over the previous year.

At the height of our praying, we found that no less than ten people were coming to know Christ each week. Our church growth has not been the result of siphoning saints from other churches. There is no need to shift the body of Christ around. We are not interested in drawing people from other churches. There are plenty of people in any given town who do not know Christ. They are the ones we're going after.

Friday: Sunday's Services and Various Church Ministries. Friday is the last day before Sunday that we meet for prayer, so we use that time to pray for upcoming services. Often we all go on a prayer walk through the church, praying for every aspect of the service. As we walk past the pulpit, we pray for the man who stands behind it on Sunday morning. In the choir loft, we pray for the choir and the director. As we walk through the pews, we pray that God will fill them with hungry souls. At one point the senior pastor challenged us to pray that God would fill the pews twice every Sunday morning. God answered that prayer so effectively that we had to start a third morning service.

We also pray for our Sunday school classes, children's church, youth group, and so forth. We encourage our pray-ers to be creative and to pray for the area of the church for which they have the greatest burden.

We have found that through this, there is a great expectancy on Sunday morning. Our pray-ers come believing God is going to do great things. There is an electricity in the air each Sunday morning because the sanctuary has been saturated with prayer. Nothing draws people to Christ more effectively than the presence of God. When the minister of music steps to the pulpit to lead the congregation in worship, there is great anticipation. As he lifts his hands and the first note is struck, there is an explosion of the presence of God!

One of our evangelism teams recently visited a couple who came to our church for the first time. They had never attended any sort of church before that. When asked what they thought of the service, they said their mouths dropped open and they stood there utterly dumbfounded as the congregation stood to worship God. They testified that there was a spirit or presence in the church that almost overwhelmed them. They knew that whatever it was that was in that service was what was missing in their lives. That night the evangelism team explained what that "Presence" was and they accepted Christ as their Saviour.

MM has been a great lesson in patience for churches that have undertaken it. The people have learned that not everyone will come to MM. Try as they might, they just can't get everyone in the church doing it. But God has always had to work with a remnant. That has never been more true than in prayer. Yet, the prayers of a few can effect many.

ALL-NIGHT PRAYER MEETING

There is more the church can offer in addition to MM. The all-night prayer meeting is a dynamic opportunity for any church congregation to gather for prayer. Our church has one such meeting on the first Friday of every month. When we began it seemed that the monthly all-night prayer meeting was going to be a perpetual experiment.

Our first such meeting was held from 10:00 p.m. to 4:00 a.m. We soon discovered that 10:00 p.m. was too late for most of our people to head out to prayer meeting. That night, we began with thirty-two people and ended with seventeen. In subsequent days, several people asked if the next meeting could begin earlier, so we met from 8:00 p.m. to 3:00 a.m. These hours proved to be much more successful, so much so that we consistently have well over one hundred people each night.

We observed some weak spots, in spite of increasing attendance. On the average we'd begin with one hundred fifty to one hundred seventy-five people, but most of them would leave by midnight. (We have always instructed our people to leave at any time they wished). The final two hours of the prayer meeting became a kind of endurance test, all of us determined to hang in there simply because none of us wanted to be call quitters.

What's more, the meeting was becoming a little dull. In chapter one of this book, we examined the powerful gatherings that were the norm during revival. Quite a contrast to those prayer meetings of yesteryear, our prayer meetings were developing into a series of spiritual want ads. We'd gather to enumerate prayer requests and then listen to someone else pray for them. Sometimes we even spent more time explaining the prayer requests than we spent praying for them. On one occasion we spent ten minutes listening to a request and no more than two minutes praying for it.

I sat in my office praying about this the day after one of our all-night prayer meetings. My spirit was deeply moved with a sense of longing for that "something" that set those first generation prayer meetings ablaze. I then recalled the prayer meetings in which I had participated in Seoul, Korea. In those prayer meetings, a message was preached first; then those gathered prayed as the Holy Spirit moved in their hearts. There was that searching soul, that crying out to God.

Again, we restructured, dealing with both of our major problems. We concluded the prayer meetings at midnight instead of 2:00 a.m. since those last two hours had become a legalistic bondage. Secondly, we modeled our meetings after those I attended in Seoul. We began much like we would for any worship service with worship and preaching. However, unlike most services, we called everyone down to the altars to pray as they felt convicted.

It was then that we began having prayer meetings that changed lives. Our people didn't have the Holy Spirit speak to their hearts only to have them nod briefly as they put on their coats and rushed home. The Holy Spirit spoke and people responded, praying, and seeking God—for the next three hours.

By all means, there is nothing wrong with protracted prayer! Many issues require extended prayer. I remember teaching a prayer seminar in Milwaukee one Friday evening during which the pastor was called out to an emergency at the hospital. One of the men from his church had arrived home from work that evening to find his wife unconscious after consuming the contents of an entire bottle of sleeping pills. The pastor arrived at the hospital just in time to hear the doctor telling the man to prepare for the death of his wife. The drugs from the pills had entered her system; it was too late to make any attempts at pumping her stomach. And her heart would not be able to continue pumping.

The pastor returned to the church as I was concluding the evening's session. As he was preparing to dismiss the meeting, he disclosed the grim facts he had heard from the doctor minutes earlier. He asked someone in the audience to lead out in prayer. We gave it a good forty-five seconds. Yet, I felt God speaking to my heart, telling me that if that woman's life was to be spared, we were not yet finished. With the pastor's permission, I told the people what I sensed in my heart and asked them to stay and pray. It was well after midnight when, as we were still praying, I sensed the spiritual battle that was taking place for her soul and how our protracted prayers were serving to build a hedge of protection around her. Then I sensed a peace in my spirit that we had prayed it through and could stop.

The next morning, as the husband entered his wife's

room, his mouth dropped open and he froze as he stared at his wife—sitting on the edge of the bed wearing a broad smile. She had been completely healed, physically, and psychologically.

We are a Church today which is over preached and under prayed. Statistics state that the average Christian prays approximately one minute each day. I don't believe any Christian sets his stop watch each day and sets out to pray for sixty seconds. Rather, it seems that we get excited about prayer and then, as the excitement subsides, gradually back away more and more until one day we realize that we have not spent a good amount of time in prayer in days or even weeks. As the Lord said to Jeremiah, "...my people have forgotten me, days without number" (Jer. 2:32).

We have strayed very far from our roots. Imagine that you and the people at your church went down to the altars and prayed for thirty minutes every Sunday night. Today we would consider that a revival. If you prayed only on that Sunday night, you would be exceeding the weekly average by more than four times. Within a month, you would have spent two hours in prayer, and within a year, you would have prayed for a total of twenty-four hours. However, during revival when churches **were** praying, it would have been said that any church spending only thirty minutes in prayer was a sickly, dying church. Yet, today the same thirty minutes would constitute a revival in our minds because of spiritual declination.

In our personal lives we have developed problems over the course of many years. There are problems which have become imbedded in the very fiber of our beings. Out of three hundred and sixty-five days, the exceptional Christian gives God only one day in prayer and then whines, "God, why haven't You changed me?"

How about you? Are you praying today about the same spiritual problems you prayed about one year ago? If so, surely you can see how you are just spinning your wheels without ever going anywhere. There is no spiritual progress.

Bear in mind that spiritual progress is directly related to the amount of time we are spending with God. Perhaps an all-night prayer meeting can be a beginning for you, a chance for you to begin praying about some of these deep-seated problems.

SERMON INTERCESSORS

Charles Spurgeon has gone down in church history as one of the greatest, most effective preachers Christianity has ever seen. One of the reasons for his success was the several hundred people who were praying for him and the service before and during it. Granted the results Spurgeon saw, sermon intercessors should be standard equipment in every church.

At our church, we have multiple morning services, so we ask that our pray-ers attend one service and pray during another in our prayer room. The intercessors pray strategically, mentioning each facet of the service as it begins. During the offering, they pray that God will move the hearts of those giving, that the needs of the church will be met, and that God will bless those giving. During the time of worship, they pray that the ministry of music will touch hearts.

Intercessors are not limited to the prayer room either. The choir members have been instructed to find prayer partners who will pray silently out in their pew as the choir is ministering. In this way, there are as many people praying as singing.

During the preaching, they pray for the preacher. They pray that his words will be anointed and that he will be under the direction of the Holy Spirit. As the service continues, they pray for whoever is in the service that the Lord might bring to their minds.

I remember an exciting experience I had during prayer one Sunday morning as we had been interceding throughout the entire service. It was a wonderful time of fellowship with the Lord, especially near the end of the service as the Spirit of God seemed to descend on us in wave after wave. It was a sovereign move of God during which everyone there could testify without hesitation that God was there. At the same time, down in the sanctuary, twelve people gave their hearts to the Lord.

Sermon intercessors are one of the most powerful vessels used in any service. It is their prayers that force Satan's hand back so that God may do what He wishes during the service. In Matthew 11:12 we read, "From the days of John the Baptist until now, the kingdom of heaven has been forcefully advancing, and forceful men lay hold of it." In no other way is force exerted as powerfully as in prayer.

I'm sure that I'll never understand why it is so hard to get God's people to pray. People want to see God move. History shows us that every time God's people sought Him, He responded in marvelous ways. Therefore, it is logical that we should pray. Yet, by and large we do not. For some strange reason, we search for other ways to accomplish the work of God.

But this is not a hard and fast rule. The best days are not necessarily behind us. For the believer who prays, the best, most exciting times with God are just ahead. We have not yet scratched the surface of God's tremendous will for us and if we faithfully pursue Him in prayer, we will do far more than just scratch that surface. For the praying pastor and lay person, the best is yet to come.